foods that don't bite back

foods that don't bite back

vegan cooking made simple

sue donaldson

arsenal pulp press

vancouver

Published in the U.S. by:
ARSENAL PULP PRESS
103, 1014 Homer Street
Vancouver, BC Canada V6B 2W9
arsenalpulp.com

The publisher gratefully acknowledges the support of the Government of Canada through the Book Publishing Industry Development Program for its publishing activities.

Edited by Jennifer Warren
Proofread by Lesley Cameron
Cover and interior design by Tanya Lloyd Kyi
Cover photograph by Jenn Walton/Digiwerx Studio
Food styling by JoAnne M. Strongman/JMS Food Styling & Design

Printed and bound in Canada

Published in Canada by Whitecap Books Ltd. (ISBN 1-55285-459-0)

The author and publisher assert that the information contained in this book is true and complete to the best of their knowledge. All recommendations are made without guarantee on the part of the authors and Arsenal Pulp Press. The author and publisher disclaim any liability in connection with the use of this information. For more information, contact the publisher.

NATIONAL LIBRARY OF CANADA CATALOGUING IN PUBLICATION DATA
Donaldson, Sue
Foods that don't bite back : vegan cooking made simple /
Sue Donaldson. — U.S.

Includes index.
ISBN 1-55152-150-4

1. Vegan cookery. 2. Veganism. I. Title.
TX837.D64.2003a   641.5'636   C2003—910297—1

contents

acknowledgements

I am grateful to many people who have aided and abetted me in the writing and promotion of this book, either in this current revised edition, or in the earlier self-published edition. First, thanks to the family and friends—too many to name—who have offered not only encouragement, support, suggestions, and recipes, but their very selves as culinary guinea pigs. (Now there's an awkward metaphor for an animal rights advocate!) Special thanks to my mom, Anne Donaldson, for teaching me most of what I know about cooking. I am also grateful to Paola Cavalieri, Holly Dean, John Donaldson, Meredith Levine, Thom Rose, Colin Macleod, Elise Moser, Roland Pierik, Karen Stacey, Christine Straehle, Elizabeth Kymlicka, and my editors at Whitecap Books for the key role each has played. And finally, thank you to Will and Codie, my partners in veganism and everything else that matters, for their boundless patience, encouragement, and love—not to mention their healthy appetites and discriminating palates.

preface

I am frequently asked to explain why I am a vegan. I am also frequently asked to pass on my favorite vegan recipes. This book is a response to both requests. Many of the recipes are borrowed and adapted. They have been garnered from a variety of sources during the 15 or so years that I have been a vegetarian/vegan, and I have given credit to the original sources where possible.

My views, too, have evolved gradually in response to much reading and many conversations. The Resources for Further Reading at the end of this book provide some indication of the reading that has shaped my ideas. I have not done my own first-hand research on topics such as veganism and health, or the living conditions of animals in modern factory farms. However, the arguments and information throughout this text are based on well-known sources and widely acknowledged and reported findings. Where the evidence is sketchy, I indicate as much. Additional research, discussion, and debate on these issues is only to be welcomed.

I have been asked, "Why not let the recipes speak for themselves?" Perhaps that would have been the wisest course, but I don't think the recipes are able to say enough. The fact that vegan food can be delicious is certainly an argument in its favor, but it is by no means the most important argument for a change of diet. That's why I'm pulling out all the stops—by giving the ethical, environmental, nutritional, *and* gustatory reasons for veganism.

what is veganism?

Veganism is a diet based on respect for the natural world, and all the creatures living in it. Vegans (pronounced vee-guns) eschew all foods and products derived from animals. In other words, they don't eat meat, chicken, or fish. Nor do they eat animal-derived foods such as eggs, milk, cheese, butter, honey, or gelatin. Nor, typically, do they use non-food products made from animals, such as leather or fur. For most vegans, this lifestyle choice reflects a desire to ground their day-to-day living in practices that are sustainable, non-exploitative, healthful, and compassionate toward all living creatures.

why become a vegan?
the ethical argument
The most important reason for becoming a vegan is to eliminate the enormous suffering inflicted on animals by modern farming practices. Most people have strong feelings about how animals should be treated. They recoil if someone kicks or otherwise mistreats a pet dog. They object to trapping methods that inflict pain on wild animals. When they see an animal in agony, they are distressed. In other words, most people think animals are capable of being harmed—by feeling pain, fear, etc. Because most people feel this way, they would never themselves abuse an animal, and think very poorly of people who do.

the realities of modern farming
And yet, the animals that we eat undergo extreme cruelty in their short lives. There are almost no laws on the books preventing cruel treatment of farm animals, and the laws that do exist are rarely enforced. The factory farm industry would be shut down overnight if it were subject to anything like the rules that govern our treatment of companion cats and dogs. Factory farm animals lead lives of misery, starting immediately after birth, when they are separated from their mothers and removed to tiny pens or cages. Their living conditions are purposely cramped to discourage movement that would burn up calories, thereby wasting feed. Most factory farm animals will live out their entire lives in these conditions, never spending a single day out of doors. They are in a state of continual frustration, unable to satisfy their basic instinctual urges (to nurse, move around, groom, build nests, select mates, and rear offspring, amongst other

things). North America has fallen far behind Europe with respect to legislation to protect farm animals. The European community enforces various regulations regarding the housing, transportation, and slaughter of farm animals. Not so in North America, where the almighty dollar reigns and farm animals are nothing more than economic units.

Factory farm chickens spend their entire lives in tiny metal cages. They are driven so crazy that they have to be de-beaked to keep them from pecking each other to death. Because they can barely move, their claws often grow to be completely enmeshed in their wire cages. In a modern chicken factory, with mechanical feeding and watering systems, one employee can "tend" thousands and thousands of chickens. It's not profitable to pay someone to actually care for the needs of individual birds. Thus, sick and ailing chickens are simply ignored and allowed to die in their cages. It's only when a condition threatens a significant proportion of the animals (and thus threatens profits) that it receives attention.

Most pigs now spend their entire lives in stalls where there isn't enough room to turn around. To facilitate cleaning, the floors of pig stalls are often made from metal slats, so that urine and feces can fall to a reservoir below. Being cloven-hoofed, pigs find the flooring extremely hard to walk on, and their feet and posture develop painful deformities. Tail docking of pigs, an extremely painful procedure, is a routine practice to keep them from biting each other's tails out of boredom and frustration.

Farm animals are selectively bred to promote meat and milk production, even though this leaves animals prone to disease and forces them to contend with awkward, distorted bodies. Many turkeys and cows, for example, can barely stand—they simply can't support their own body weight. There have even been efforts made to breed pigs that are born blind so they won't be distracted from the business of fattening up. This is an awful demonstration of a mentality that views farm animals as nothing more than machines for converting grain to meat to money.

Animals make the trip to the slaughterhouse in horribly crowded conditions, often in extreme heat or cold. Many don't survive the journey. (Once again, this seems perversely wasteful on the part of the industry, but it's actually not. The cost of better conditions for all the animals outweighs the calculated loss of some of them.) Most beef cattle spend their last days or weeks on feed lots attached to a slaughterhouse. They are castrated (so they'll put on more weight) and de-horned (because conditions are so crowded that they would accidentally gore one another otherwise). These procedures are regularly performed without anesthetic, causing excruciating pain. The animals' food supply is cut off once it is calculated that they won't have time to turn it into usable meat before slaughtering. The animals are gradually herded toward the slaughterhouse through a series of walkways and holding pens. They panic because they can smell the blood, hear the cries, and sense the terror of animals further down the line. They have to be prodded mercilessly to move along.

When the moment of death comes, it is not necessarily painless, or instantaneous. Slaughtering methods differ widely, but one popular method is to kill cows by electrocution. It was once believed that this was a painless death, because while death doesn't come instantly, it was thought that consciousness and sensation were immediately extinguished. However, the use of electrocution to execute human beings was stopped when it was discovered that this is not the case. Electrocution causes a kind of paralysis—so the human or animal can't give any outward sign of distress—but sensation and awareness may in fact continue until death is achieved. A more humane method is to use a "captive-bolt pistol" to instantly stun an animal unconscious, but it's more expensive than other methods and hence avoided by many slaughterhouses.

Many people have heard about the cruelties involved in the veal industry—day-old calves are taken from their mothers and put into tiny stalls where they can't move, even to turn their heads to lick and groom themselves. They are kept in darkness to reduce their restlessness, resulting in blindness in most of the calves. They spend four months this way and are then slaughtered. Veal is prized for its tenderness (lack of muscle) and whiteness, so movement is completely restricted to prevent the development of muscle, and the animals' diet is deliberately iron-deficient to induce anemia. The calves develop an insatiable craving for iron, so their stalls are made from wood to prevent access to any rusting metal parts. They are denied solid food or anything to suck on. They can't be given bedding because they would eat it in their desperation to find a balanced diet.

The treatment of veal calves is particularly appalling, but it is hardly an anomaly in farming practice. Rather, it is one end of a continuum that involves endless cruelties inflicted on animals. The treatment of animals in modern factory farms is governed by profit, pure and simple. Unfortunately, the most profitable practices don't usually involve humane treatment of animals. In the frequent instances where the factory farming industry can benefit financially from ignoring the comfort, happiness, and health of the animals, it does so, quite ruthlessly.

Defenders of factory farming argue that it's not in their economic interest to abuse animals. They say, "The animals are eating, so they must be happy." But how many humans do you know who stop eating when they are bored, depressed, and anxious? Intensive livestock farming denies animals the opportunity to engage in all those activities—wandering, running, ruminating, grooming, scratching, flying, procreating, caring for their young—that they exhibit in natural surroundings. Eating is all they have left.

dairy farming

Unfortunately, it is not just animals destined to become meat that are subject to appalling practices. Vegetarians who eat dairy products are still implicated in an industry that harms and exploits animals, an industry that is just as much controlled by the ruthless demands of the profit motive. The living and breeding conditions of layer chickens and dairy cows are designed to maximize egg and milk production, not the well-being of the animals. Layer chickens are de-beaked and live out their lives in tiny wire cages. They are worn out after about two years under conditions designed to overstimulate egg production (although their natural life span is about 15 years). When egg production starts to fall off, they become chicken soup. Dairy cows aren't yet reared under the intensive conditions that other farm animals are, although trends are moving in that direction. Dairy cows are impregnated continuously to keep them producing milk. The male offspring are slaughtered or turned into veal calves. Females become future dairy producers. The natural life span of a cow is about 25 years, but dairy cows are worn out within four or five years, at which point they are dispatched to the rendering plant (where they are boiled down to become animal "by-product"). Throughout their lives, animals in the dairy industry are injected with a steady stream of hormones and antibiotics to increase production and to fight off the diseases to which they become prone under unnatural and unhealthy living conditions.

Given the enormity of suffering caused by the factory farming industry, it's hard to understand how people can continue to eat meat and dairy products. Most people try not to think about it too much. But when pushed to do so, here are some of the rationalizations they turn to.

do animals suffer?

One strategy is to deny that animals can be harmed. On this view, when we get upset about seeing a dog being beaten or a half-dead deer suffering beside the road, we are just being sentimental—projecting suffering onto animals that they don't really feel. Sure, they may exhibit signs of suffering, such as panic, crying out, and aggression. Perhaps they are sentient, yes, but not in the way that humans are. Their consciousness simply isn't sophisticated enough. They don't have the language, knowledge, or understanding that humans do, and these are the mental capacities that give pain and suffering their full horror. Some people cling to this view, despite the evidence of animals' non-verbal behavior indicating that they do suffer, and despite the physiological and genetic evidence of similarities between their sensory systems and our own.

But those who claim to hold this "unsentimental" view must consider the full implications of such a position. They draw a line between human and non-human animals' capacity for suffering on the basis of the possession of advanced mental capacities—language, knowledge, understanding, etc. However, there are many humans who don't possess these advanced mental capacities, such as babies and infants, people with profound mental handicaps or brain injuries, and people who have lost mental function due to the degenerative diseases of old age. It's true that infants have a sensory system (as do animals) and that they respond to certain stimuli in ways that suggest they actually do suffer (as do animals), but it would be sentimental of us to project onto them a kind of suffering that only fully capacitated human beings are able to feel. Should we therefore ignore the apparent pain of infants? This is the appalling, but logical, conclusion of arguing that it is safe to assume that animals don't suffer because they can't directly tell us that they do.

Nobody is happy defending this position. So the next strategy is to say, "Well, I know they suffer, and it's terrible, but humans have to eat. Animals eat one another, and we eat animals. That's life: 'Nature, red in tooth and claw.'" But this argument doesn't hold up to scrutiny. First of all, humans don't need to eat meat. Humans are true omnivores—able to draw on a huge variety of foods to meet our nutritional needs. In fact, our obsession with eating meat has had disastrous implications for our health and the environment. We would be better off without it. There are many vegan creatures in the world. Humans have the option of being so, and thereby reducing the amount of suffering in the world. One of the beauties of human social and cultural development is that we have learned ways other than "the law of the jungle" to conduct our affairs. The fact that nature can be terrifying and cruel doesn't mean that we need to pile it on. We can eliminate suffering where possible, even if there will always be plenty left over.

It is interesting to note how often defenders of meat-eating try to have it both ways. First, they argue that it's okay for humans to exploit other animals because our capacity for culture and moral decision-making places us on another plane. When they lose this argument, they retreat to the old saw that humans are just animals with natural instincts (e.g. eating meat), which we cannot be expected to control. Which will it be? Are we, or are we not, creatures capable of transcending mere biological drives, of thinking morally, and conducting our behavior in accordance with this thinking?

the "consistency" argument

This brings us to another point. Some people agree that becoming a vegan is the right thing to do, but they don't think they are up to it. They can imagine cutting out meat, but never dairy products; or they can imagine being a vegan at home, but don't see how they could possibly manage every time they go out. They worry that because animal by-products and animal testing are used in so many daily items (leather, glues, drugs, toiletries), it's almost impossible to be consistently ethical. And if you can't be consistent, what's the point of bothering at all?

The point is that however much we cut back on eating animals, this represents a small but real elimination of suffering in the world. The idea that if we can't be consistent we might as well give up doesn't make sense. Our responsibility is to keep trying, not to achieve perfection. Just because I have a bad day and yell at my child doesn't mean I throw in the towel on parenting. I get up the next day and try again. Nor would anyone stop feeding their own children because it seems pointless to care for a few individuals when so many others are starving. Likewise, the fact that we can't save all of the animals doesn't mean we shouldn't save the ones we can.

the "priorities" argument

At this point the meat-eater might concede that becoming vegetarian, in theory, is the right thing to do. But, he or she protests, there are many things one ought to do, and it's not possible to do them all. There is enormous suffering in the world, and we are faced with a sort of triage situation—too little time and too few resources to meet all needs. We must establish priorities—and by far the most important goal is to alleviate human suffering. The suffering of animals is unfortunate, but it's not as terrible as human suffering. When we've improved the lot of humans, that will be the time to turn our energies to the abuse of animals. People who hold this view say things like, "Well, I'm more concerned about *human* suffering," as though concern for humans and non-human animals were somehow mutually exclusive.

This is a multiply perverse viewpoint because it implies that being a vegan reduces the time available to care for humans. While it's true that, on first becoming a vegan, there is some start-up time required to learn new recipes, we are not talking about a significant time investment here, especially with the recent explosion in vegan recipe books and foods. And once you've made the transition, it takes no more hours in the day to eat plants than it does to eat animals.

cruelty to animals hurts us all

In any case, it's a false dichotomy to begin with. The fact is, meat-eating is bad not just for animals, but for humans and for the planet too. Caring for humans means caring about human health and the environment. It means caring about sustainable and efficient agricultural practices that would allow us to feed everyone on the planet, rather than funneling resources to produce meat for the more affluent. One-third of the world's grain harvest is fed to animals. Were it directed to humans instead, we could feed the billion people who suffer from chronic hunger. Caring about humans means being alarmed by a land-hungry cattle culture that is forcing peasants and indigenous peoples off their lands all around the globe, reducing them to poverty and dependence. It means caring about the process of desertification and the resulting famines that cost countless lives in sub-Saharan Africa. It also means caring about the awful working conditions of those who work in slaughterhouses. Of all occupations, slaughterhouse workers have the highest turnover rate (and the second-highest rate of injury after loggers). Nobody does this kind of work if they have an option. In North America, slaughterhouse workers are drawn overwhelmingly from the desperately poor, recent immigrants, and migrant workers. The high turnover rate has made it extremely difficult to organize strong and effective unions.

One final connection between animal and human interests concerns the mounting evidence of a link between violence toward animals and violence toward human beings. It seems that people who are inclined to be callous toward animals display the same inclination vis-à-vis humans. Indeed, they often desensitize themselves to violence by first "practicing" on animals. Our ability to love and to empathize—to put ourselves in the shoes of another—is a general capacity, not one that stops at the border of our own species. And so, as our treatment of farm animals becomes more and more inhumane, we should be concerned about how this behavior hardens the human heart more generally.

In light of all this, it's clear that the humanitarian reasons for becoming a vegan are overwhelming. I would hope that the plight of animals would be sufficient to motivate anyone. But in any case, no meat-eater should take comfort in the pretense of placing a higher priority on the well-being of humans. The interests of humans and animals are not in competition here.

Perhaps there is one sense in which human "interest" does compete with the interests of animals, and that is the human interest in eating animals for the pure pleasure of it—pleasure in the taste of meat, in the associated rituals, in the desire to wear leather and fur accessories—and in the convenience of doing things the way one has always done them. Pleasure and tradition—the same arguments used by aficionados of bullfighting (or cockfighting). Most meat-eaters would prefer not to be placed in that company, but they are. They don't directly inflict torture on animals, but neither do the spectators at a bullfight. Meat-eating is an inherited cultural practice, and it's hard to step back from a practice you've grown up thinking is normal. It's much easier to look at other cultures and condemn their cruelties. The real challenge is to look at our own cultural practices, and subject them to critical reappraisal.

the "free-range" alternative

I should address one final issue regarding the moral status of animals and their capacity to suffer. Many people say that they object to the cruel treatment of animals, but not to the killing and consumption of animals per se. In other words, if it were possible for farm animals to live a natural, pleasant sort of life, and

then be killed without pain and suffering, that would be acceptable. I agree that such a system would be vastly preferable to what we have, although I still don't think it would be a morally acceptable system. Animals have an interest in living without pain and suffering, just like humans. They also have an interest in living for the sake of living. They instinctively avoid situations that might lead to death. But beyond an instinctive tendency to choose life, do they not actually value their lives? To me, the answer is clearly yes. Animals take pleasure in living—just picture a dog racing through a field, or playing ball, or enjoying a snooze in the sun. Animals' lives have value in and of themselves, independent of any value they might afford to humans. And so, even if it were possible to raise and then slaughter animals in a humane way, I wouldn't want to sacrifice animals simply to satisfy a human desire to eat meat when a vegan option is available. Of course, in times and places where a healthy vegan diet isn't possible, a humane system of raising or hunting animals for meat or dairy might be the best we can do. For most of us, however, a healthful vegan diet is perfectly accessible, and therefore eating animals cannot be justified.

I don't think there is any such thing as "cruelty-free" meat. But for people making the transition to veganism, switching to organic or free-range meats is sometimes a first step. It's a very small step. "Free-range" meats may be clearly superior from a health point of view, but it is not clear how much difference the system makes from the animals' perspective. Animals sold as "free-range" still, for the most part, spend much of their lives in confined spaces. They still lead short lives. They are still transported under unregulated conditions. And they still end up at the slaughterhouse. Standards vary considerably from one operation to the next, so consumers who go the "free-range" route should ask their supplier lots of questions about how the animals have been treated. But wouldn't it be better to put all that energy into embracing veganism?

the environmental argument

Adopting a vegan diet is one of the most important steps an environmentally conscious individual can take. The methods and scope of modern livestock farming take an enormous toll on the environment, including rainforest destruction, inefficient use of arable land, excessive consumption of energy and water, and the production of agricultural pollutants. Farming hasn't always been this destructive. Traditional livestock farming was (and is, where still practiced) more efficient and sustainable than contemporary practices in many ways.

saving the land

Good agricultural land was once reserved for raising crops for human consumption. Farm animals grazed on marginal land for much of their food, thereby making efficient use of land that couldn't raise crops. Availability of grazing land acted as a control on livestock numbers, and meat from domesticated animals was a supplement to, not the centerpiece of, the human diet.

Today, most of the crops grown in the U.S.A. (and one-third of grain crops produced worldwide) are destined to feed livestock, not humans. This is a grossly inefficient way to use arable land. It takes about 10 times as much land to feed a person on a meat-based diet as opposed to a plant-based one. In other words, the same land that feeds 10 people eating grains, legumes, fruits, and vegetables, feeds only one person when the land is used to produce feed for beef cattle.

The great thirst of the livestock industry for grazing territory and for land to raise crops for animal feed has led to the degradation of land worldwide. The once "Great Plains" of North America are plagued by soil erosion, as are the banks of its rivers and streams. The native flora and fauna in a vast area have been annihilated by "hoofed locusts," an apt expression coined by author Jeremy Rifkin to capture the devastating effect of cattle ranching. In Africa, a relentless process of desertification continues as forests and once-productive agricultural land make way for livestock-grazing and monoculture. In Central and South America, vast tracts of the rain-forest have been destroyed in order to provide grazing land for cattle. Because the rainforest rests on a very thin layer of topsoil, exposing this by deforestation leads to severe erosion, resulting in land that is unsuitable for agriculture. Meanwhile, the enormous bio-diversity of the rainforest is lost, as is its critical role in cleaning the atmosphere by transforming CO_2 into oxygen.

conserving resources

In addition to wasteful and destructive land-use practices, livestock farming hurts the environment in other important ways. A great deal of energy is consumed to heat barns and to operate modern farm technol-ogy. Livestock farming also requires vast water consumption for feed crops and for the animals. Indeed, over 50 percent of the water con-sumed in the U.S.A. can be traced to livestock farming. It is estimated that 15 times as much water is required to produce one pound of beef protein compared to an equal amount of vegetable protein.

agricultural pollutants

Livestock farming is also a serious source of environmental contami-nation. Fertilizers, herbicides, and pesticides used in the production of feed crops build up on the land and run off into streams and rivers, where they poison the natural ecology. Fertilizers also emit nitrous oxide, a contributor to the greenhouse gas problem. Add to this the methane emissions from cattle and the carbon dioxide pro-duced by the vast burnoff of the rainforest (estimated to be the source of one-third of all carbon dioxide emissions) and the overall contribution of livestock farming to global warming is considerable. And finally, there is the enormous amount of waste produced by animals, which often makes its way untreated into lakes and rivers, disrupting the natural ecology and posing a serious health risk. Each year in the U.S.A., farm animals produce 1 billion tons of waste. In Canada, a major offender is the intensive pig farming industry, which has expanded rapidly in recent years and produces vast amounts of waste. Pig operations are causing an uproar in many small communities confronted by the stench and surface water contamination.

The North American farm and food industry is working hard to export an animal-based diet to the rest of the world, with some success. This is a disastrous trend, with serious consequences for human health and the environment. Rather than exporting our fixation with meat and dairy, we should be re-learning the benefits of traditional diets that place less emphasis on animal foods and make a sustainable use of resources possible.

responsible choices

If you are concerned about the environment, there are a number of dietary steps you can take to demonstrate your concern. The single most important step is to become a vegan. Only by drastically limiting our dependence on animal-based foods can we develop a sustainable relationship with the environment. Another key step is to buy organic produce whenever possible, thus encouraging the agricultural industry to lessen its dependency on chemicals. A further benefit of going organic is that you thereby support what are typically small, family-run farms over agribusiness. Large-scale and intensive farming is responsible for most environmental degradation. Many small farmers feel they have been forced to adopt destructive practices in order to compete, and wish they had more options. Conscientious choices by consumers could help reverse this economic imperative. A third step you can take to help the environment is to buy local foods as much as possible, thereby minimizing the amount of energy used in the storage and transportation of food. And finally, be a demanding consumer. Ask your grocer to label foods adequately so that you know where they come from. And ask the government to implement food labeling regulations so we all know which foods have been certified organic, and which foods have been irradiated, treated with hormones, or genetically engineered.

In many parts of North America and Europe, it is possible to follow a vegan diet that relies heavily on locally grown and organic plant foods. If you live in the more remote and northern areas, however, there are going to be trade-offs. For example, if you don't have access to locally grown organic produce, is it better to buy imported organic food or locally grown non-organic food? You are faced with a difficult choice. Meanwhile, you can pressure local grocers and growers to offer a local organic option. Others face more difficult choices. For example, in the far north, is it better to be a vegan, eating produce primarily imported from the south, or to adopt a more meat-centered diet based on local hunting and trapping? From a strictly environmental point of view, the answer is almost certainly the latter. There are some situations, therefore, where environmental considerations might conflict with the moral and health reasons for choosing a vegan diet. For most of us, however, the environmental choices are clear. The meat and dairy foods consumed by most North Americans are the product of intensive livestock farming, not sustainable hunting and trapping practices. The environmental costs of modern factory farming are enormous, and so the responsible environmental choice is to become a vegan.

the health argument

Many people express concerns about the healthfulness of a vegan diet, which is so different from the mainstream North American diet that it is often labeled "extreme" and "misguided." And yet, ironically, concern for health is precisely the reason why so many others have turned to veganism in recent years. The typical North American diet—high in animal fats, cholesterol, and protein, and low in complex carbohydrates and dietary fiber—has been implicated in a host of "Western" diseases such as heart disease, colon and breast cancers, stroke, diabetes, appendicitis, kidney stones, osteoporosis, and arthritis. For many years now, health professionals, including the Heart and Cancer Associations, have consistently recommended that we lower our consumption of saturated fats and cholesterol and increase our consumption of fruits, vegetables, and dietary fiber. In other words, we should all eat more like vegans.

guidelines for a healthy diet

Forty to fifty percent of calories in the average North American diet come from fat, most of it saturated animal fat. The World Health Organization recommends a total fat intake of between 15 and 30 percent of calories. As important as reducing total fat intake is replacing unhealthy fats like saturated animal fat, cholesterol (found only in animal foods), and trans fatty acids (common in fast foods and processed foods like crackers and cookies) with good fats like olive oil, omega 3 fatty acids (e.g. flax seed oil), and naturally occurring fats from nuts, seeds, avocados, and olives.

On an animal-centered diet, it is difficult to lower total fat intake to recommended levels unless you stick to low-fat dairy products and lean cuts of meat (eaten on occasion, not at every meal), and cook and consume them without adding much additional fat (by steaming, not frying, and by foregoing gravies and sauces). Moreover, meat-eaters have to be wary of eating foods like avocados, nuts, or omega 3-based salad dressings because these foods would add more fat to an already fat-heavy diet, whereas vegans can consume these healthful foods regularly and still maintain total fat consumption within recommended levels.

Nutritional guidelines urge us to make vegetables, fruits, legumes, and whole grains the cornerstones of our diet. A minimum of 55 percent of our calories should come from complex carbohydrates, and only 10 to 15 percent of our calories should come from protein. The typical North American diet (high in fat and protein, low in complex carbs) cannot be adapted to the guidelines simply by tinkering a little here and there (by eating vegetarian a couple of times per week, for example). A much more fundamental change is required. A vegan diet, on the other hand, measures up very well against the guidelines, incorporating all the suggestions the experts have been urging on us for years. On a vegan diet, your cholesterol consumption is automatically reduced to zero. Fat intake is easily limited to 20 percent of calories, and consists primarily of healthy fats. Consumption of fruits, vegetables, and dietary fiber increases by leaps and bounds. And there is no need to monitor your diet on a daily basis, carefully counting fat or fiber intake, because the decision to eliminate animal products ensures the overall change in diet required.

It is strange that a vegan diet is labeled "extreme," given that it's closer to traditional patterns of consumption than the heavily meat- and dairy-focused diet of industrialized Western nations. Two-thirds of the world's population eat a mostly plant-based diet, consuming on average just 10 percent of their protein from animal sources (versus 70 percent in the West). Despite the fact that a heavily meat- and dairy-focused diet represents a significant deviation from traditional eating patterns, people persist in their fears that vegans must be undernourished. The most common worry is that vegans can't possibly get enough protein. Another concern is: if vegans eliminate dairy products, then how can they possibly get enough calcium? And finally, many people wonder about pesticide exposure from eating too many fresh fruits and vegetables. All three of these concerns represent serious misunderstandings about vegan diets and nutrition, and as they are frequently repeated I will address each of them here.

pesticide residues on fruits and vegetables

Let's begin with the issue of pesticide residues in food. There is an ongoing debate about the safety of chemically grown foods. Governments keep adjusting the "safe levels" for chemical residues, and tests repeatedly indicate that many foods (especially imported produce) exceed these levels. Many people believe that toxic residues in food are implicated in certain cancers, allergies, and autoimmune diseases, and until we know for sure, it seems prudent to try to limit our exposure to these chemicals. A simple step is to wash fruits and vegetables carefully, especially if the outer peels or skins are to be eaten. You might want to curtail your consumption of certain foods, such as tomatoes, which have been found repeatedly to contain very high levels of pesticide residues. Buying certified organic produce is the best way to reduce exposure to pesticides, and to pressure the industry to adopt safe practices. It is also important for consumers to demand clear and informative labeling practices so they know how produce is grown, how far it has traveled, and whether or not it has been subject to irradiation or genetic engineering.

Buying organic not only limits exposure to chemical residues, it also means that you are buying more nutritious food. Conventional farming is geared toward producing foods that are fast-growing, pest-resistant, and durable. The process of selective breeding has lengthened growing seasons and shelf life, but these changes have come at the expense of nutritional content. Lengthy storage, transportation, and refrigeration further contribute to nutritional losses. (To give one small example, broccoli that has been refrigerated for two days loses 34 percent of its vitamin C content.) For all of these reasons, it makes sense to buy locally grown, organic foods.

Concerns about the safety of fruits and vegetables are legitimate, but it is terribly misguided to think we can avoid these problems by eating meat and dairy products. When we eat meat, we are eating all of the pesticides and other toxins that the animal and its food supply have been exposed to. Cows are fed crops produced by chemical farming, and when a cow eats feed containing pesticide residues, the pesticides are stored up and concentrated in the cow's flesh. The concentration of poisons increases as one moves up the food chain. Livestock are now commonly fed meat by-products in conjunction with, or in lieu of, grains. This places them even higher up on the food chain. The pesticides used on feed crops become concentrated in the flesh and organs of the animals that eat them. When the animals are slaughtered and the rendered by-products are fed to other chickens, pigs, or cows, the toxins are concentrated even further. (Another result of the practice of substituting animal by-products for traditional feed is the transmission of diseases such as mad cow disease amongst animals, and into the human diet.)

The chemicals and viruses that animals ingest with their feed are stored up and passed along the food chain. Meat-eating humans, at the top of this food chain, ingest all the poisons concentrated at lower levels. (Just as fish, high on the aquatic food chain, become reservoirs for toxins such as mercury, PCBs, and other water pollutants.) It is not just the animal's flesh that is affected. Pesticide residues are also found in cow's milk, as are residues from antibiotics and hormones with which cows are routinely treated. Thus, neither meat nor dairy products offer a haven from the pesticides and other chemicals so endemic to modern farming. On the contrary, their bodies become toxic storage depots. And so, if you want to limit your exposure to chemical residues in food, substituting meat and dairy products for vegetables is simply jumping from the frying pan into the fire. Indeed, the U.S. Environmental Protection Agency estimates that 90 to 95 percent of the pesticides in our diet come from meat, fish, and dairy products. The best course is to eat low on the food chain (i.e. plants) and to eat organically grown foods where possible.

the protein and calcium myths

We can now turn to another myth about the alleged dangers of a vegan diet. How do vegans get adequate protein? Actually, a vegan diet poses no serious challenges here. We tend to overestimate the amount of protein required for a healthy diet. Average protein consumption is about 25 percent of calories, whereas the recommended allowance is only 10 to 15 percent. Indeed, there is mounting evidence that overconsumption of animal protein contributes to health problems, such as osteoporosis. One of the by-products of animal protein digestion is a sulfur-containing amino acid that the body neutralizes by binding it with calcium and excreting it through the kidneys. The more animal protein we eat, the more calcium must be leeched from our bodies' reserves—our bones. The high incidence of osteoporosis in North America is due to a variety of factors (e.g. consumption of alcohol, caffeine and salt, smoking, lack of exercise, and genetic factors), but diets high in animal protein are thought by many to be a contributing factor.

It used to be claimed that vegans had to carefully combine different kinds of foods at every meal to ensure adequate protein consumption. Not true. Plant protein is not inferior to animal protein. Plant foods like tofu, tempeh, and other soy foods provide all the essential amino acids (the building blocks of protein), just like meat. Indeed, the amino acids found in meat originate in plant sources. Cows eat grains that become beef protein; fish eat seaweed that becomes fish protein. As long as you eat a reasonably varied diet and get enough calories, it is easy to consume sufficient protein on a vegan diet. Vegans derive some protein from almost all the foods they eat (including many vegetables and whole grains), but real protein powerhouses include tofu and other soy foods, as well as beans, nuts, and seeds. It is recommended that vegans eat two—three servings of these foods per day. (Examples of one serving would be: 3 Tbsp. [45 mL] peanut butter; or $1/4$ cup [60 mL] seeds; or $1/2$ cup [120 mL] tempeh; or one veggie burger.)*

Vegans are also frequently asked about calcium. The dairy industry has indoctrinated us to believe that unless we eat dairy products, our calcium intake must be inadequate. And yet, in parts of the world where people do not consume dairy products (such as China), people do not suffer from calcium deficiency. Indeed, it is the countries with the highest dairy consumption—North America, Scandinavia, Western Europe—that have the highest rates of osteoporosis in the world! So where do vegans get this critical nutrient? Luckily, there are many excellent plant sources, including dark leafy greens (kale, collards, broccoli, bok choy), almonds, tahini, seaweed, tofu, beans (especially soy, white, navy, and black turtle beans), and

*Dietary recommendations are from *Becoming Vegan: The complete guide to adopting a healthy plant-based diet,* by Brenda Davis and Vesanto Melina.

calcium-fortified foods like soymilk and orange juice. Vegans should get six—eight servings per day of these calcium-rich foods. (Examples of one serving would be: 1 cup [240 mL] cooked greens; or $1/4$ cup [60 mL] almonds; or 1 cup [240 mL] beans; or $1/2$ cup [120 mL] fortified soymilk or orange juice).* We have been brainwashed to see cow's milk as the ultimate calcium source, but when you think about it, where did the cow get all that calcium that enriches her milk? From eating her greens! And the added bonus of vegan sources of calcium is that they don't come packaged with the negatives of dairy products; namely fat, a total absence of fiber, and, for many people, indigestibility.

dietary concerns for vegans

There are two dietary concerns that vegans should keep in mind: ensuring adequate sources of vitamins B_{12} and D. For B_{12}, vegans should incorporate foods like nutritional yeast and B_{12} fortified foods like soymilk and soy-based meat alternatives into their diets. Additional supplementation may also be good idea. I have my B_{12} levels checked by the doctor periodically, and have never had any problems even though I rarely take supplements. However, B_{12} is such a vital nutrient that it's best not to take any chances.

Vitamin D requirements can be met with approximately five minutes of sun exposure each day. This vitamin can be stored up, so slightly longer exposure on sunny days provides an adequate amounts to carry one through overcast days. However, in parts of the world that have long winters with low amounts of sunlight, vitamin D supplementation is a good idea. Most soymilks and rice milks are fortified with vitamin D, just as cow's milk is, so you don't need to worry about additional supplementation provided you eat these fortified foods.

embracing the vegan alternative

Why are North Americans so convinced that meat and dairy products are essential to their diet? The producers of these foods have sub-

---

*Dietary recommendations are from *Becoming Vegan: The complete guide to adopting a healthy plant-based diet,* by Brenda Davis and Vesanto Melina.

jected us to a barrage of misleading nutritional information. It's true that animal foods are an excellent source of protein. They also contribute some important vitamins to the diet. However, protein is only one factor in a well-balanced diet, and one that has been overemphasized in the typical North American diet. Meat and dairy products are not well-rounded foods. They provide protein, but they are high in saturated fat and provide no dietary fiber. Plant foods, on the other hand, are not only an excellent source of protein and vitamins; they are also low in fat and high in fiber, thus providing a much better match for human dietary needs.

We read every day about the extraordinary health benefits of eating more fruits and vegetables. These foods deserve to be the mainstay of our diet, not to be relegated to a side dish. No one should be dissuaded from a plant-based diet by outdated myths about protein and calcium consumption. The Physicians Committee for Responsible Medicine advises us to re-orient our diet to the new four food groups: whole grains, vegetables, fruits, and legumes. A vast literature and body of scientific evidence attests to the healthfulness of a well-balanced vegan diet centered on these foods. In the face of this evidence no one can claim, in good conscience, to eat meat and dairy products out of concern for health. Health concerns should lead us to embrace, not reject, a vegan diet.

raising vegan children

In this section, I have been primarily concerned with addressing some of the most common health myths that lead people to dismiss a vegan diet. In this overview of vegan nutrition, I have not addressed the dietary needs of infants, pregnant women, and others with special dietary concerns. It is quite possible to follow a meatless diet under these circumstances, as generations of Buddhists, Hindus, Seventh Day Adventists, and other vegan or vegetarian cultures can attest. But you do need to do your homework and prepare for opposition. Parents are particularly vulnerable to propaganda about what they should feed their children, and as a result, there are serious misconceptions about what constitutes a healthy diet for children. For example, some people will express great alarm at the prospect of not giving children cow's milk. In fact, the high fat and protein content of cow's milk is designed for calves, not human children. The nutritional composition of cow's milk and human milk differs significantly. (For example, cow's milk has three times as much protein.) Furthermore, many children are lactose-intolerant (unable to digest cow's milk) and have been made seriously ill by the general misconception that cow's milk is a health food, and indispensable for growing children.

If you are considering raising a child on a vegan diet, it is advisable to consult a knowledgeable dietician. This will provide you with peace of mind regarding your child's nutritional needs, as well as helpful ammunition for winning over critics (such as day care providers, teachers, and other parents) who will undoubtedly raise questions about your child's diet. The books and websites listed in the Resources for Further Reading provide some guidance for parents of vegan children, and supply additional references. In particular, *Becoming Vegan: The complete guide to adopting a healthy plant-based diet,* by Brenda Davis and Vesanto Melina, is an indispensable guide, as is the website of the Physicians Committee for Responsible Medicine (www.pcrm.org). Look for books and other resources that not only answer your questions about nutrition, but also provide practical tips for meeting the challenge of raising vegan kids in a non-vegan world.

tips on the transition to veganism

It would be hard to overstate the benefits of switching to a vegan diet. It's great for our health. It revitalizes our relationship with food. And most importantly, it eases our consciences, which suffer from our participation in the gross cruelties of modern factory farming. If we lived in a vegan culture, it would be much easier to opt for a vegan diet. But daily bombardment by advertising, restaurant menus, and shopping aisles continually reminds us of what we have given up. The thought of eating meat now disgusts me, but will the time ever come when I'm not tempted by cheese or whipped cream? Sometimes I give into temptation. In our family we call these occasions "moral holidays." I wish I didn't have to take them, but for me, they are the corollary of being self-disciplined most of the time. You will find your own strategies, your own manageable "fit" for doing the best you can in an imperfect world. Don't be distracted by your slip-ups—who was it who said consistency is the hobgoblin of little minds? Just keep focused on the big picture.

managing the transition

The prospect of changing from a meat-based to a vegan diet can be overwhelming, but only if you imagine that it has to be effected overnight. The key for most people is gradual change. Begin by eliminating red meat, then moving on to chicken, and so on. Or begin by eating vegan one day per week, and gradually building up. Assume that it might take several months to make a complete change. This will give you time to experiment with new recipes, and it will give your body time to adjust to new foods (especially the increased amount of fiber in your diet). A great variety of prepared and semi-prepared vegan foods (too many to mention!) are available these days at health food stores, and most grocery stores too. These can be a great help.

A gradual transition period also gives your extended family and friends time to adjust. It is important to let others know that you are serious about making a change, and to give them strategies to cope. When you're invited for dinner, explain that you are a vegan, and offer to bring one or two dishes. A traditional meat-based diet tends to include lots of plant foods, and the key to coexisting with meat-eaters is to focus on the foods that you eat in common—grains, vegetables, etc. The most helpful thing your non-vegan family and friends can do is to keep meat and plant foods separate during food preparation and presentation. Boiled eggs, caesar dressing, and bacon bits are common accompaniments to a green salad, but there are plenty of vegan alternatives. Steamed vegetables can be flavored with margarine or olive oil, rather than butter. Vegetable stock, wine, or tamari can be substituted for meat stocks when simmering, sautéeing, or stir-frying. Cheese and cream sauces can be avoided, or you can experiment with substitutes such as tofu cheeses, lemon-tahini sauces, soymilk-based white sauces, and so on.

Ask friends and family to develop the habit of making vegetable dishes purely vegetable. That way, when you join them for a meal, most of the dishes can be shared in common. They might have an additional meat dish on the side. You might bring along a bean or tofu dish. Bring plenty so you can expose your meat-eating friends to vegan alternatives. One of the great pleasures of becoming a vegan is this opportunity to introduce others to a new cuisine. You will hear the exclamation, "I had no idea vegetarian food could be so delicious," over and over again. The key is that if friends and family are willing to compromise somewhat in their preparation of plant foods, then the specter of preparing completely separate meals can be avoided.

Having said this, some vegans face great hostility to their diet, regardless of how tactfully they present the situation. Food is at the heart of family rituals, and change is threatening. As noted above, gradual change is one strategy for overcoming hostility. Another is to do lots of your own cooking/entertaining. Introduce family and friends to your new diet on your turf, rather than expecting them to make too many changes too quickly to the way they cook. Another strategy is to compromise—e.g., to agree to eat turkey once or twice a year if that preserves a family tradition (and family peace). If you face constant criticism, or attempts to undermine your resolve, the best strategy is to refuse to rise to the bait. Be firm, be consistent, be patient.

keeping your eye on the big picture

One of the challenges you will face as a vegan is that it is very difficult to follow the diet consistently. When you want to eat out, one strategy is to make arrangements with the restaurant ahead of time. Many restaurants are happy to accommodate special diets if they're given some warning. You needn't restrict yourself to vegetarian restaurants. Lots of traditional diets (Indian, Middle Eastern, Italian) offer abundant vegan alternatives. But be realistic about the fact that you won't always manage. Situations will arise—when you're traveling, when you're a guest—in which you will either have to compromise or go without food. You may have explained your diet to someone in advance, but they didn't completely understand, or you may simply be in a situation where it is impossible to know exactly what you are eating, or how it was prepared. I would say, do the best you can, and don't worry about it. As I argued earlier, the goal isn't to be 100 percent consistent in a quest for perfection. The goal is to do what you can. The fact that you might occasionally have to eat a cheese sandwich or a soup made with chicken stock does nothing to detract from the fact that, most of the time, you have been able and/or willing to be a vegan.

vegan friends and rituals

Any time you adopt a new discipline or lifestyle—whether it's an exercise regime, a diet, a commitment to read more, or a new hobby—fellow travelers can make the transition a whole lot easier, and lots more fun. Seek out other vegans and get together to cook with them now and then. If you can't find any through your own network of friends and colleagues, check out the Internet, or look up your local vegetarian society in the phone book. In most cities there are potlucks and other events that bring vegans together to share and celebrate their lifestyle.

It's important to develop rituals and traditions around your new foods to replace those you have given up; otherwise change will simply feel like deprivation. In our family, we are evolving rituals around eating foods in season—savoring cabbage and root vegetable stews or soups through the winter; asparagus, fiddleheads, and baby greens in the spring; and the full glory of the harvest through summer and early autumn. We don't eat strictly in season, but more and more we are opting to eat organic, locally grown, seasonal foods—for our health, for the environment, and for the excellent flavor. Eating this way, you naturally develop rituals around the first and last fresh corn of the season, or raspberries, or giant, end-of-season zucchinis. You also develop a relationship with local farmers and evolve your own small rituals around going to the market.

That's all very well, you may say, but what about those times when *nothing* is in season? There are, of course, various methods for preserving foods. Freezing is an excellent method of preserving nutritional value as well as the flavors you can't live without during the long winter months. Here are a couple of tricks you might not have tried. When the basil harvest is at its height, buy great quantities and put it through the food processor, combined with a bit of salt and oil. This semi-pesto freezes well, and preserves the taste of fresh basil in an incredibly compact form. I also buy lots of red peppers when they are plentiful and cheap, roast them, and freeze them for later use in pastas, soups, and dips. I don't grow many vegetables, but I do have a large herb garden (*anybody* can grow herbs successfully). I bring annuals, such as dill, parsley, and basil indoors and nurse them as long as I can through the winter. I harvest armfuls of perennials such as tarragon, sage, savory, oregano, and thyme and hang them to dry from the pantry ceiling. Non-hardy perennials, like bay and rosemary, I keep in pots outdoors for six months, and sitting on a sunny windowsill the rest of the time. Fresh herbs go a long way toward sprucing up those winter meals when fresh vegetables are scarce. The small amount of space and effort required to grow them is amply rewarded. As you become more familiar with vegan cuisine, you will discover a handful of versatile flavor enhancers— herbs and spices, roasted peppers and garlic, caramelized onions, toasted nuts and seeds, balsamic vinegar, toasted sesame oil, tamari, fruit juices and peels, maple syrup—that form the foundation of a varied, year-round, and delicious vegan cuisine.

hidden animal ingredients

Many foods that might seem vegan at first glance in fact contain animal ingredients. Whey (a milk by-product) shows up in many crackers, breads, and other baked and processed goods. Lard (saturated animal fat) is used in many baked goods, though less so than a few years ago. Gelatin (a meat by-product) is a popular thickener in many desserts, and a component of Jell-O and marshmallows. Animal-derived vitamin D_3 is used to fortify many brands of margarine (but vegan brands are available at natural food stores). I could go on. If you want help deciphering food labels, go to the Vegan Resource Group's indispensable website: www.vrg.org/nutshell/faqingredients.htm.

Vegans vary considerably in their adherence to the vegan ideal of avoiding all animal-derived foods and products. Some vegans eat honey. Some use animal-derived pharmaceutical products. Some are strict vegans at home, but more flexible when traveling, and so on. Most vegans see themselves as aspiring toward an ideal, not as having achieved it. In fact, in a non-vegan world, it's very difficult to completely avoid the use of animal-derived products. Glues, videotape, and vitamin supplements are just a few of the many products where hidden animal-derived ingredients may lurk. And food labels don't tell the whole story, either. Sometimes a food that doesn't contain animal products in itself nonetheless uses animal products in the production process. For example, animal bones are sometimes used to filter sugar. And fish gelatin is used to filter wine and beer. So it's challenging to be a strict vegan. Luckily, though, it's getting easier all the time. Recent years have seen an explosion in the availability of vegan products such as non-leather shoes, vegan recipe books, vegan "fast foods," vegan organic wines, and vegan websites packed with useful products and information (see the Resources for Further Reading at the end of this book).

Like many vegans, I am a work in progress. I have only recently eliminated honey from my diet. I still use white sugar and drink wine despite the animal by-products used in processing. I frequently buy margarine even if it is fortified with animal-  derived vitamin D_3 instead of plant-derived D_2. And I eat many foods in restaurants (e.g. bread) without ensuring that they are free of animal ingredients. So I am far from a "pure" vegan. But then, purity isn't the goal. The goal is to live as compassionately as possible, to do the best you reasonably can, and to inspire others by example. To eliminate 99 percent of the animal products from your life is a readily doable and significant accomplishment. It's a goal any of us can attain. There are some people who will find the time, energy, and discipline to go the distance and eliminate that last 1 percent. I applaud them. (These are the individuals who will pressure manufacturers to clarify labeling practices and to provide the completely vegan alternatives that make life easier for the rest of us.)

But I am also wary of being too focused on the quest to eliminate every trace of animal by-product from daily life. It's the big picture that matters: the goal of weaning society in general off its animal-food dependency. I'd rather focus my energies on social change than on the elusive quest for individual purity. I don't want to alienate potential vegans by emphasizing the challenge and discipline required to avoid every last animal ingredient. I want to encourage them by demystifying veganism, by showing how achievable it is, and how good it feels.

Veganism as an individual dietary choice must be placed in a larger social context, a context that inevitably implies certain compromises and trade-offs. Every vegan, or aspiring vegan, will balance these trade-offs a little differently. And that's okay. We don't need to follow the exact same path—providing we're all headed in the same direction, and providing we all keep moving to make room for the others coming up behind.

vegan substitutions for cooking and baking

Non-vegan ingredient:	Vegan substitute:
cow's milk	soymilk or rice milk
yogurt	soy yogurt
cottage or ricotta cheese	mashed medium/firm tofu
butter	oil or margarine
1 egg	1 tsp. (5 mL) egg replacer or 1 Tbsp. (15 mL) ground flax seed + 3 Tbsp. (45mL) water
gelatin	agar-agar
beef or chicken stock	vegetable stock or water mixed with miso or tamari
honey	maple syrup (or rice syrup, which is less sweet, so increase amount by one-third)
white sugar	cane juice granules
chocolate/chocolate chips	dairy-free dark chocolate/ chocolate chips

breakfast tips

Many standard breakfast foods are vegan—fruits and juices, grains and breads. A variety of soy yogurts are available, and many people enjoy soymilk or rice milk as a topping for cereals. Maple Cream (p. 132) makes a delicious and protein-rich topping for fruit or granola. Check out the options at your local grocery or health food store. There are innumerable vegetarian "sausage links," "breakfast bacons," etc. available. Non-dairy pancake mixes are plentiful. And there are mixes that simply require the addition of tofu to make vegan "scrambled eggs." For weekends, or a special brunch, I usually make fruit salad, Banana-Poppyseed Muffins (p. 135), and one or both of the recipes that follow:

fried potatoes with mushrooms and garlic (Serves 4)

6 medium potatoes

3 Tbsp. (45 mL) olive oil

1 cup (240 mL) white mushrooms, sliced

1 onion, sliced

2 cloves garlic, minced

salt and pepper to taste

Peel and quarter potatoes, and boil them until just tender. Slice and set them aside. Heat the oil over medium heat in a large frying pan and sauté the mushrooms, onion, and garlic. When soft, add the potatoes and salt and pepper. Stir-fry until the potatoes are golden.

tempeh strips with maple syrup (Serves 4)

1 240 g (8$\frac{1}{2}$ oz) package tempeh, thawed

$\frac{1}{2}$ Tbsp. (7.5 mL) olive oil

$\frac{1}{2}$ cup (120 mL) vegetable stock

1 Tbsp. (15 mL) tamari

$\frac{1}{3}$ cup (80 mL) maple syrup

Cut the tempeh in half. Then, using a sharp knife, slice each half through the middle to make two thin layers. Heat the oil in a skillet and brown the tempeh on both sides, adding additional oil if necessary. Add the stock, cover the skillet tightly, and steam the tempeh until the liquid is almost absorbed. Add the tamari and cook until the pan is dry. Transfer the tempeh to a cutting board and slice it into thin strips. Brush lightly on both sides with maple syrup. Reheat on the grill or under the broiler.

lunch tips

There are a variety of prepared and semi-prepared vegan food products available at your grocery or health food store. These can be a real help in the lunch department. Try making sandwiches with vegetarian "pepperoni," veggie burgers, or non-dairy "cream cheese" products. Spreads such as tahini, hummus, and baba ghanoush are great in a pita sandwich, or used as a dip for pita wedges or raw vegetables. And tofu wieners are practically indistinguishable from the real thing. There is tremendous variety in all of these products, so don't give up if you don't like the first one you try.

Some of the recipes in this book make delicious leftovers for lunch. For example, Tarragon Lentil-Nut Loaf (p. 88) or Korean Tofu (p. 104) are excellent in sandwiches. And Stuffed Grapevine Leaves (p. 80) are easy to pack for lunches or picnics. Two additional recipes for satisfying and nutritious sandwich fillings follow.

carrot-tahini sandwich filling (Makes 4 sandwiches)

- 4 medium carrots, finely grated
- $\frac{1}{4}$ cup (60 mL) tahini
- 2 Tbsp. (30 mL) eggless mayonnaise
- 2 Tbsp. (30 mL) nutritional yeast
- 2 Tbsp. (30 mL) diced green onion (optional)

Combine all ingredients.

(Adapted from Brenda Davis, Victoria Harrison, and Vesanto Melina's Becoming Vegetarian.)

grilled tempeh sandwich filling (Makes 2 sandwiches)

- 1 240 g ($8\frac{1}{2}$ oz) package tempeh, thawed
- $\frac{1}{2}$ Tbsp. (7.5 mL) olive oil
- $\frac{1}{2}$ cup (120 mL) vegetable stock
- 1 Tbsp. (15 mL) tamari
- lettuce, tomato, and other condiments

Cut the tempeh in half. Then, using a sharp knife, slice each half through the middle to make two thin layers. Heat the oil in a skillet and brown the tempeh on both sides, adding additional oil if necessary. Add the stock, cover the skillet tightly, and steam the tempeh until the liquid is almost absorbed. Add the tamari and cook until the pan is dry. Use it warm or cold as a sandwich filling, adding lettuce, tomato, and other condiments as desired.

Variation: Prepare the tempeh as above, then brush it with your favorite barbecue or other sauce, and grill or place briefly under the broiler.

starters

kalamata olive tapenade

This earthy-flavored dip is a most often-requested recipe. It is admittedly a nuisance to pit the olives, but once that's done it takes less than 5 minutes to whip up this recipe in the food processor. (Serves 6—8)

1 1/2 cups (360 mL) whole black kalamata olives, pitted
1/4 cup (60 mL) whole almonds
2 Tbsp. (30 mL) fresh parsley
1 Tbsp. (15 mL) capers, drained
2 cloves garlic
zest from one orange
1 1/2 tsp. (7.5 mL) fennel seeds
1/4 cup (60 mL) olive oil

Combine all ingredients, except oil, in a food processor. Process until the mixture is coarsely chopped. With the machine running, gradually add oil; process until fairly smooth. Serve with crackers or baguette.

(Adapted from a recipe that appeared in Gusto!, Oct. 1995)

white bean and herb spread

Sage has to be the most underused herb (though not in this recipe collection, as you will discover). Its pungent flavor is a welcome accompaniment to vegan cuisine. (Serves 4—6)

1 14 oz. (398 mL) can navy beans, drained and rinsed
1 ½ Tbsp. (22.5 mL) lemon juice
15 large leaves fresh sage
2 cloves garlic
¼ cup (60 mL) olive oil
½ tsp. (2.5 mL) salt
pepper to taste

Place half of the beans in a small bowl. Mash roughly. Place the remaining beans, lemon juice, sage leaves, and garlic in a food processor. Process. Add the olive oil and salt. Process until smooth. Add the processed mixture to the mashed beans and mix well. Add pepper to taste. Serve with crusty bread.

pecan mushroom pâté

This is a rich and filling appetizer. It looks nice served in individual ramequin dishes, but if they aren't available just make one large pâté in a small loaf pan or ovenproof dish. (Serves 10)

6 oz. (170 g) silken tofu
½ cup (120 mL) pecans
6 medium shiitake mushrooms caps, sliced (save stems for soup stock)
1 cup (240 mL) white mushrooms, sliced
1 Tbsp. (15 mL) vegetable oil
1 small leek (white and light green parts only), sliced
1 ½ Tbsp. (22.5 mL) sherry
1 Tbsp. (15 mL) tamari
1 Tbsp. (15 mL) fresh parsley
1 Tbsp. (15 mL) fresh tarragon
salt to taste
sprigs of fresh tarragon for garnish

Preheat the oven to 350°F (175°C). Drain the tofu on a paper towel to remove excess moisture. Meanwhile, toast the pecans in a dry pan over low to medium heat until lightly toasted. Set aside. Sauté the shiitake and white mushrooms together in ½ Tbsp. (7.5 mL) oil over medium-high heat until lightly browned. Set aside. In the same pan, add the remaining ½ Tbsp. (7.5 mL) oil and sauté the leek over medium heat until soft. In a food processor, combine all ingredients and process until very smooth. Taste for salt. Press into four rame-quin dishes (½ cup [120 mL] size), or other ovenproof dish. Bake for 30 minutes. Cool, then chill overnight. Garnish the pâté with a fresh sprig of tarragon and serve with crackers or baguette.

crostini with roasted peppers and garlic

This colorful appetizer is all about the essence of garlic. It's a bit messy, though, so have napkins at the ready. And note that the peppers need to be prepared and marinated in advance. (Serves 6)

2 red bell peppers
1 yellow bell pepper
5 cloves garlic, peeled
$1/_3$ cup (80 mL) olive oil
1 baguette
fresh basil for garnish (optional)

To roast the peppers: cut them in halves or thirds and remove the seeds. Flatten the peppers somewhat to even out the surface and place them skin side up on a broiling pan. Grill them under the broiler until the skins are really blackened. Place peppers in a paper bag and let them sweat for 10 minutes. The skins will peel off easily; discard the skin. Slice the peppers into thin strips and place them in a small bowl. Slice 3 cloves of garlic thinly. Add the garlic slices and olive oil to the peppers, stirring so everything is mixed and coated with oil. Cover and refrigerate for several hours (or overnight), but remove from the fridge an hour before serving to bring them back up to room temperature.

To serve: Preheat the oven to 350°F (175°C). Cut the remaining two cloves of garlic in half. Set aside. Slice the baguette in $1/_2$ in. (1.2 cm) slices, on a slight angle to increase the surface area. Lay the pieces of bread on a baking sheet in a single layer. Toast them in the oven for 5–10 minutes, until lightly toasted. Rub each toast with garlic by grasping a half clove in your fingers, cut side down, and scraping it firmly across the entire top surface of the bread. When the garlic starts to disintegrate, switch to a new clove. Place the toasts on a serving tray. Remove the garlic slices from the peppers and discard. Spoon the peppers and oil over the toasts, and garnish with basil leaves if desired. Serve immediately.

fennel and apple phyllo triangles

If you've never worked with phyllo pastry, it's time to have a go. It's easy to use and incredibly versatile. These phyllo triangles make an elegant appetizer. Serve them warm, on a small plate decorated with orange slices and sprigs of fennel tops. (Serves 8)

> 8 sheets of vegan phyllo pastry, thawed
> $\frac{1}{2}$ Granny Smith apple (or other sharp apple), cored and diced
> $\frac{1}{2}$ Gala apple, (or other sweet apple) cored and diced
> $\frac{1}{2}$ head fennel, thinly sliced
> 1 leek, white part only, sliced
> $\frac{1}{4}$ cup (60 mL) golden raisins
> 1 Tbsp. (15 mL) olive oil, plus extra for brushing
> zest of 1 small orange, grated
> $\frac{1}{4}$ tsp (1.2 mL) salt
> pepper to taste

Cover the pastry with a damp cloth to keep it from drying out. Preheat the oven to 350°F (175°C). Mix together all other ingredients in a small bowl. Take the first sheet of pastry and fold it in half lengthwise, brushing lightly with olive oil. Place $\frac{1}{8}$ of the filling at base of sheet. Fold the bottom left corner of the sheet over to the right side (making a triangle shape over the filling). Brush lightly with oil. Continue folding phyllo, brushing at intervals, until you reach the top of the sheet. Seal the outside with another light brush of olive oil and place on a baking sheet. Repeat with the remaining 7 phyllo sheets. Bake the triangles for about 20 minutes, until golden.

note:
Triangles can be prepared a few hours ahead, carefully covered with plastic wrap, and then baked just before serving.

(Adapted from a recipe that appeared in Gusto!, Oct. 1996)

artichokes with herb vinaigrette

The perfect ice-breaker appetizer. Steamed artichokes are a bit messy to eat, somebody is bound to need directions about what parts to eat, and how, and everyone ends up rubbing elbows over the dipping bowl. Creative chaos. (1 or 2 per person)

1–2 artichokes per person

juice of $\frac{1}{2}$ lemon per artichoke, plus 1 Tbsp. (15 mL) for pot

$\frac{1}{8}$ cup (30 mL) olive oil per artichoke

salt and pepper to taste

$\frac{1}{4}$ tsp. (1.2 mL) mixed herbs per artichoke

To prepare the artichokes, pull off a couple of layers of outer leaves. Then trim off the tops of the artichokes (approximately the top third, to remove sharp tips). Rub the tops in lemon juice. Trim the stems to about 1 in. (2.5 cm). Peel the stems (including the rough section at the base of the artichoke leaves), and dip them in lemon juice. Bring a large pot of water to a boil. Add 1 Tbsp. (15 mL) lemon juice. Boil the artichokes for about 15 minutes, until tender. Serve with a dipping mixture of olive oil and lemon juice generously seasoned with salt, fresh pepper, and herbs if desired.

How do you eat an artichoke? Pull off a leaf and dip the base in vinaigrette. To eat it, scrape the pulp from the base of the leaf with your teeth and discard the remainder of the leaf. As you work your way through the artichoke, the leaves become more tender and edible. When you reach the center, there will be a little furry-looking section. Remove this and discard, and you are left with the incredibly delicious heart, which can be eaten in its entirety.

soups

gazpacho

The quintessential summer soup. If you like it smooth, whiz everything in the food processor. If you prefer it crunchy, dice the cucumber by hand. (Serves 6)

1 28 oz. (796 mL) can crushed tomatoes
1 large English cucumber, peeled
1 clove garlic, peeled
3 cups (720 mL) tomato juice (or vegetable cocktail)
1 red bell pepper, seeded and minced
4–5 scallions, minced
juice of 1 lemon
2 Tbsp. (30 mL) red wine vinegar
2 Tbsp. (30 mL) olive oil
1 ½ Tbsp. (22.5 mL) sherry
2 tsp. (10 mL) rice syrup
1 tsp. (5 mL) each dried tarragon and basil
dash of tabasco sauce
dash of cumin
salt and pepper to taste

Process the crushed tomatoes, cucumber, and garlic in a food processor until smooth. Combine with the remaining ingredients in a large bowl and chill for at least 2 hours.

chilled cucumber soup

Another refreshing summer soup. Don't be tempted to add more garlic,
though. It will continue to develop as the soup chills. (Serves 5—6)

2 large English cucumbers, peeled, seeded, and chopped
2 cups (475 mL) water
2 cups (475 mL) soy yogurt
$^1/_4$ cup (60 mL) packed, fresh mint leaves
1 Tbsp. (15 mL) rice syrup
1 small clove garlic, peeled and coarsely chopped
2 tsp. (10 mL) salt
chives or mint leaves for garnish

Combine all ingredients, except chives, in a food processor. Chill
several hours or overnight. Garnish with chives. Serve chilled.

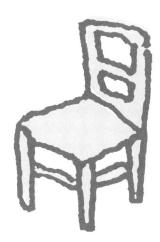

hungarian mushroom soup

This rich, satisfying soup can be either a starter or a meal in itself served with bread and salad. It also makes a heavenly sauce. Simply reduce the stock to 1 cup (240 mL) and voilà, you have the perfect topping for Tarragon Lentil-Nut Loaf (p. 88), potatoes, or rice. (Serves 4)

2 Tbsp. (30 mL) olive oil
2 large onions, sliced very thinly
4 cups (950 mL) white mushrooms, sliced
2½ cups (600 mL) vegetable stock
1 Tbsp. (15 mL) sweet paprika
1 Tbsp. (15 mL) tamari
2 tsp. (10 mL) dried dill weed
2 Tbsp. (30 mL) margarine
2½ Tbsp. (37.5 mL) flour
1 cup (240 mL) soymilk
2 tsp. (10 mL) lemon juice
salt and pepper to taste

Heat the olive oil in a medium saucepan over medium heat. Lightly salt the onions and sauté for a few minutes. Add mushrooms, ½ cup (120 mL) stock, paprika, tamari, and dill. Stir. Cover and simmer 15 minutes. Melt the margarine in a small saucepan. Add the flour and whisk for a few minutes. Add the soymilk. Cook, stirring frequently, over low heat for 5—10 minutes until thick. Stir in the remaining 2 cups (475 mL) stock and stir thoroughly. Then add to mushroom mixture and stir thoroughly. Cover and simmer 10—15 minutes. Just before serving, add the lemon juice, and salt and pepper.

(Adapted from Mollie Katzen's Moosewood Cookbook.)

almond-split pea soup

I am grateful to Elizabeth Kymlicka for this unusual dish. The almond essence lends this soup a distinctive flavor, which works best served in modest portions as a starter. (Serves 4)

4 cups (950 mL) water
2 large onions, chopped
1 cup (240 mL) yellow split peas
2 tsp. (10 mL) almond essence
1 $\frac{1}{2}$ tsp. (7.5 mL) salt
minced parsley and sliced roasted almonds for garnish

Combine the water, onions, and split peas in a medium saucepan and cover. Bring to a boil, and then simmer on medium-low heat until split peas are soft (about 45 minutes). Purée the mixture in a blender or food processor. Add the almond essence and salt. Reheat, garnish, and serve.

garlic bread soup

This is another delicious but rich soup that works best as a starter. It's a snap to make (10 minutes). (Serves 4)

1 cup (240 mL) blanched almonds
2 slices white or whole wheat bread
3 cups (720 mL) vegetable stock
3–4 cloves garlic, peeled
3 Tbsp. (45 mL) olive oil
2 Tbsp. (30 mL) rice vinegar
$\frac{1}{2}$ tsp. (2.5 mL) salt
croutons (optional)

In a small, dry pan, roast the nuts over low to medium heat until lightly browned. Set aside. In a small bowl, drizzle the bread with $\frac{1}{2}$ cup (120 mL) stock. Let sit for a moment. Then squeeze out the bread and discard the stock. Grind the nuts, bread, and garlic in a food processor. Transfer to a small saucepan. Add remaining $2\frac{1}{2}$ cups (600 mL) stock, olive oil, vinegar, and salt. Reheat, stirring occasionally. Garnish with croutons if desired.

spicy root soup

This works well as both a starter and a main course. The spicy ginger flavor and vibrant orange color are delightfully warming on a cool day. (Serves 4)

1 large onion, sliced thinly
1 Tbsp. (15 mL) olive oil
3$\frac{1}{2}$ cups (840 mL) carrots, peeled and chopped (or substitute parsnips
    for up to $\frac{1}{3}$ of total)
3 cups (720 mL) vegetable stock
2 tsp. (10 mL) fresh ginger, grated
$\frac{1}{2}$ tsp. (2.5 mL) ground coriander
$\frac{1}{4}$ tsp. (1.2 mL) nutmeg
1$\frac{1}{2}$ cups (360 mL) soymilk
salt to taste
croutons (optional)

In a medium saucepan, sauté the onion in oil over low-medium heat until soft. Add carrots, stock, ginger, coriander, and nutmeg. Bring to a boil. Reduce heat and simmer for 30 minutes. Purée the soup in a blender or food processor. Return to the saucepan. Add the soymilk and reheat gently. Add salt to taste. Serve garnished with croutons.

variation:
When adding soymilk, also add $\frac{1}{2}$ cup (120 mL) orange juice and $\frac{1}{2}$ cup (120 mL) minced fresh cilantro.

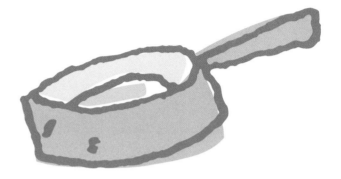

side dishes

grilled summer vegetable salad

This salad composé provides a wonderful combination of colors, textures, and flavors. The fresh vegetables are a light and crunchy counterpoint to the richer, more robust grilled vegetables.
(Serves 4–6)

4 cups (1 L) baby salad greens
$\frac{1}{2}$ cup (120 mL) balsamic vinegar
2 Tbsp. (30 mL) olive oil, plus extra for brushing
10 fresh basil leaves
salt and pepper to taste

A combination of the following grilled vegetables (4 cups [1 L] total):
eggplant, sliced
red or yellow sweet peppers, cut in half, seeds removed
zucchini, sliced
mushrooms
green onions
asparagus

A combination of the following fresh vegetables (1 cup [240 mL] total):
tomatoes, sliced
cucumbers, sliced
radishes

A combination of the following boiled or steamed vegetables
(2 cups [475 mL] total):
green beans
potatoes, sliced
beets, sliced
carrots, sliced

To grill/roast vegetables under the broiler: Eggplant, mushrooms, green onions, asparagus, and zucchini should be lightly brushed with olive oil and grilled under the broiler. Turn once, grilling until tender and nicely browned.

To roast red peppers: Flatten pepper halves somewhat for a more even surface. Grill them under the broiler until skins are really blackened. Place peppers in a paper bag and sweat them for 10 minutes. The skin will peel off easily. Discard the skin and slice the peppers.

Spread the baby greens evenly on a large salad platter. Arrange the grilled, fresh, and steamed vegetables on top in rows or groupings. Sprinkle the entire platter with fresh basil leaves. Combine balsamic vinegar, 2 Tbsp. (30 mL) olive oil, and salt and pepper to taste. Then drizzle it over the vegetables.

avocado and roasted fennel salad

Crunchy, fresh fennel is lovely in salads, but roasting brings out a whole other dimension. When cherry tomatoes are in season, you might prefer to substitute them for the avocado. (Serves 4)

2 large fennel bulbs, tops and outer layer removed
$\frac{1}{4}$ cup (60 mL) olive oil, plus extra for brushing
2 Tbsp. (30 mL) balsamic vinegar
1 clove garlic, minced
$\frac{1}{2}$ tsp. (2.5 mL) salt
ground pepper
5 cups (1.2 L) firm salad greens (e.g. romaine or iceberg)
1 small ripe avocado, peeled and cut into large wedges

Preheat the oven to 375°F (190°C). Cut each fennel bulb into 10 wedges. Brush them lightly with olive oil. Spread them out on a baking sheet sprayed with non-stick vegetable oil. Roast 35—45 minutes, until lightly browned and tender. Remove and cool. Prepare the vinaigrette by whisking together the olive oil, balsamic vinegar, garlic, salt, and pepper. Toss the fennel with vinaigrette in a large bowl. Add the salad greens and avocado and toss gently. Serve immediately.

potato-artichoke salad with maple-mustard vinaigrette

Be sure to toast the sunflower seeds thoroughly. They are a lovely contrast to the other ingredients. If you're not serving the salad immediately, leave the sunflower seeds aside to preserve their crunch. (Serves 4)

3 cups (720 mL) new potatoes, scrubbed but unpeeled

2 cups (475 mL) yellow wax beans

1 14 oz. (398 mL) can artichoke hearts

$^1/_4$ cup (60 mL) fresh dill, chopped

$^1/_4$ cup (60 mL) raw sunflower seeds

$^1/_4$ cup (60 mL) olive oil

1 $^1/_2$ Tbsp. (22.5 mL) Dijon mustard

1 $^1/_2$ Tbsp. (22.5 mL) apple cider vinegar

1 Tbsp. (15 mL) maple syrup

$^3/_4$ tsp. (4 mL) salt

Cover potatoes with water in a medium saucepan. Bring to a boil, then simmer until the potatoes are just tender. Drain, cut into bite-sized pieces, and set aside. Steam or boil the beans until they are tender-crisp. Drain, cut into thirds, and set aside. Drain and rinse the artichokes. Cut into bite-sized pieces. Combine with the potatoes, beans, and dill in a serving bowl. Lay the sunflower seeds in the bottom of a small frying pan. Cook over low-medium heat until the seeds are lightly toasted. Add the seeds to the vegetables. Prepare the vinaigrette by whisking together the olive oil, mustard, vinegar, maple syrup, and salt. Pour over the vegetables and mix well.

sweet potato and pecan salad with lime vinaigrette

This salad is a bit time-consuming for every day, but well worth the effort to impress company. The lime juice balances the richness of the other ingredients in this wonderfully eye-catching dish. (Serves 4)

2 medium sweet potatoes, scrubbed but unpeeled
2 Tbsp. (30 mL) olive oil
$\frac{1}{2}$ red bell pepper, seeded and cut in strips
$\frac{1}{2}$ cup (120 mL) red onion, sliced thinly
1 tsp. (5 mL) mustard seeds
pinch each of cayenne, cinnamon, and ground cumin
$\frac{1}{3}$ cup (80 mL) pecan halves
2 Tbsp. (30 mL) lime juice
$\frac{1}{2}$ tsp. (2.5 mL) toasted (dark) sesame oil
$\frac{1}{2}$ tsp. (2.5 mL) salt
$\frac{1}{4}$ cup (60 mL) fresh cilantro, roughly chopped, for garnish

Preheat the oven to 375°F (190°C). Cover the potatoes with water in a large pot. Bring to a boil and simmer for 15 minutes. Drain, then slice them into $\frac{1}{2}$ in. (1.2 cm) rounds. Coat a large baking dish with 1 Tbsp. (15 mL) olive oil. Arrange the potatoes, red pepper, and onion in the dish, and bake for 15 minutes, or until tender. Meanwhile, sauté the spices in 1 Tbsp. (15 mL) olive oil for 2 minutes. Add the pecans and sauté 2 minutes longer, until brown. Remove the vegetables from the oven, and drizzle them with lime juice and sesame oil. Sprinkle with salt. Toss with the spicy pecan mixture. Let sit for 15 minutes before serving, and garnish with cilantro.

(Adapted from a recipe that appeared in Gusto!, Dec. 1996)

broccoli and cauliflower medley

A great buffet salad inherited from my grandmother. Kids like it thanks to the super-sweet dressing (an effective strategy for getting them to eat their cruciferous vegetables). Take an extra minute to really cut the broccoli and cauliflower into small pieces; it makes all the difference. (Serves 8—10)

DRESSING:

$\frac{1}{2}$ cup (120 mL) sugar

$\frac{1}{2}$ cup (120 mL) white vinegar

$\frac{1}{2}$ cup (120 mL) olive oil

1 Tbsp. (15 mL) Dijon mustard

1 Tbsp. (15 mL) grated red onion

SALAD:

1 bunch broccoli, cut into bite-sized pieces

1 small head cauliflower, cut into bite-sized pieces

1 red onion, sliced very thinly (before slicing, grate and set aside
   1 Tbsp. [15 mL] for dressing)

$\frac{1}{2}$ cup (120 mL) slivered almonds, lightly toasted

Whisk the dressing ingredients together. Combine the broccoli, cauliflower, and sliced onion in a large bowl. Drizzle the dressing over the vegetables and marinate, in the fridge, for 4 hours minimum. Stir the vegetables regularly to re-coat with dressing. Add the almonds just before serving so they stay crunchy.

mexican corn salad

A zesty accompaniment to chili or tacos. Or practically a meal in itself!
(Serves 4)

2 cups (475 mL) cooked corn (preferably fresh, but not necessary)
1 14 oz. (398 mL) can black beans, drained and rinsed
1 avocado, diced
1 large tomato, diced
$\frac{1}{2}$ cup (120 mL) fresh cilantro, chopped
3 Tbsp. (45 mL) lime juice
3 Tbsp. (45 mL) olive oil
3 cloves garlic, minced
1 jalapeno pepper, seeded and minced
salt to taste

Combine all ingredients and
let the flavors fuse for at least
1 hour. Serve chilled or at
room temperature.

thai noodle salad

Thank you to Louise Noble for sharing her favorite potluck salad. Add a loaf of crusty bread and you've got a meal. (Serves 4)

SALAD:

$\frac{1}{2}$ lb. (225 g) spaghetti or large, flat rice noodles

2 cups (475 mL) baby spinach

1 $\frac{1}{2}$ cups (360 mL) grape tomatoes, sliced in half

1 medium carrot, peeled and julienned

$\frac{1}{2}$ red bell pepper, seeded and sliced in thin strips

$\frac{1}{2}$ cup (120 mL) fresh cilantro, chopped

DRESSING:

3 Tbsp. (45 mL) lime juice

2 Tbsp. (30 mL) toasted (dark) sesame oil

1 $\frac{1}{2}$ Tbsp. (22.5 mL) fresh ginger, grated

3 cloves garlic, minced

1 $\frac{1}{2}$ Tbsp. (22.5 mL) tamari

1 Tbsp. (15 mL) rice vinegar

1 Tbsp. (15 mL) sugar

1 $\frac{1}{2}$ tsp. (7.5mL) chili paste

Cook the noodles until al dente. While they are cooking, whisk together the dressing ingredients. Rinse and drain the noodles thoroughly and place them in a large bowl. Add half of the dressing to the noodles and stir gently until noodles are coated. Add the fresh vegetables and the remaining dressing and stir to combine. Let sit for $\frac{1}{2}$ hour. Serve at room temperature.

tabouleh

This classic Middle Eastern dish is refreshing and surprisingly filling. It makes a handy picnic or potluck salad. An interesting variation is to replace the tomatoes with strawberries. (Serves 4–6)

1 1/2 cups (360 mL) boiling water
1 cup (240 mL) bulgur
1 1/2 tsp. (7.5 mL) salt
1/2 cup (120 mL) packed, fresh parsley
1/4 cup (60 mL) packed, fresh mint leaves
1 clove garlic, peeled
1/4 cup (60 mL) lemon juice
1/4 cup (60 mL) olive oil
1 small cucumber, peeled and diced
2 tomatoes, diced
salt and pepper to taste

Combine the boiling water, bulgur, and salt in a bowl. Cover and let stand for 15 minutes. Mince the parsley, mint, and garlic in a food processor. Add the minced herb/garlic mixture, lemon juice, and olive oil to the bulgur and mix thoroughly. Chill for at least two hours. Just before serving, add the cucumber, tomatoes, and salt and pepper to taste.

wild rice waldorf salad

Fruity, crunchy, tangy—with the tantalizing fragrance of cardamom. A wonderful addition to any buffet. (Serves 6)

SALAD:

1 1/2 cups (360 mL) wild rice/brown rice blend

1/4 cup (60 mL) slivered almonds

1 large Granny Smith apple, diced

3 Tbsp. (45 mL) fresh lemon juice

1 red bell pepper, seeded and diced

1 cup (240 mL) celery, diced

1/2 cup (120 mL) red onion, minced

1/2 cup (120 mL) currants

DRESSING:

1/2 cup (120 mL) orange juice

1 Tbsp. (15 mL) olive oil

1 Tbsp. (15 mL) maple syrup

1 tsp. (5 mL) ground coriander

1/2 tsp. (2.5 mL) ground cardamom

Prepare the rice according to package directions. Do not overcook. Place the almonds in a small frying pan and toast them over low to medium heat until lightly browned. Toss the apple with lemon juice in a large bowl. Add the pepper, celery, red onion, currants, and toasted nuts. Set aside. Whisk together all of the dressing ingredients. Combine all ingredients in a large bowl, and toss well to combine. Serve at room temperature or chilled.

(Adapted from the Moosewood Collective's Moosewood Restaurant Low-Fat Favorites.)

asparagus with ginger and orange

A simple preparation is best for fresh asparagus—lightly steamed, seasoned with salt and pepper, and drizzled with oil or dotted with margarine. However, by the second week of asparagus season you might be ready to try something a little different… (Serves 4—6)

25—30 spears fresh asparagus
$\frac{1}{4}$ cup (60 mL) olive oil
4 tsp. (20 mL) fresh ginger, grated
juice of 2 oranges
2 tsp. (10 mL) toasted (dark) sesame oil

Trim the asparagus spears and peel them approximately halfway up each spear. Heat the olive oil in a large frying pan over medium heat. Add the asparagus and ginger. Sauté, stirring, until the asparagus is coated with oil and ginger. Add the orange juice. Cover and simmer until the asparagus is tender. Toss with sesame oil and serve.

baked red peppers with garlic and capers

These baked peppers maintain their form well, making them an elegant and colorful side dish. They should be very juicy, so don't stint on the olive oil. (Serves 4)

2 red bell peppers
2 medium tomatoes, quartered
4 tsp. (20 mL) capers, drained
2 cloves garlic, sliced thinly
8 tsp. (40 mL) olive oil
fresh basil leaves for garnish (optional)

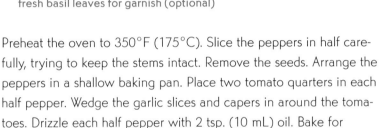

Preheat the oven to 350°F (175°C). Slice the peppers in half carefully, trying to keep the stems intact. Remove the seeds. Arrange the peppers in a shallow baking pan. Place two tomato quarters in each half pepper. Wedge the garlic slices and capers in around the tomatoes. Drizzle each half pepper with 2 tsp. (10 mL) oil. Bake for 40—50 minutes, until tender. Garnish with basil and serve.

ratatouille

I make this dish all summer long, but especially during corn season. A meal of fresh bread, ratatouille, and corn on the cob—how better to celebrate the harvest? (Serves 6)

2 Tbsp. (30 mL) olive oil

2 large onions, sliced very thinly

4—6 fresh tomatoes, chopped

1 small eggplant, diced

2 zucchinis, diced

1 red bell pepper, seeded and diced

1 yellow bell pepper, seeded and diced

4 cloves garlic, minced

1 Tbsp. (15 mL) dried basil

2 tsp. (10 mL) sugar

1 tsp. (5 mL) each dried oregano and thyme

1 tsp. (5 mL) salt

Heat the oil in a large frying pan over medium heat. Sauté the onions until soft. Add the remaining ingredients and stir until the tomatoes start to release their juices. Cover and simmer for 30 minutes, adding a splash of water or tomato juice if the ratatouille starts to get dry.

roasted vegetables provençal

Savor the aromas of the Mediterranean on a cold winter day. For variety, try adding other vegetables—zucchini, sweet potatoes, carrots, or pitted black kalamata olives—to the potato, garlic, and onion base. Don't be alarmed by the amount of garlic; baking it mellows the flavor. (Serves 4)

4 medium potatoes, peeled and cut into small bite-sized pieces
1 large red onion, peeled and cut into large chunks
8–12 cloves garlic, peeled
$\frac{1}{2}$ Tbsp. (7.5 mL) olive oil
2 tsp. (10 mL) dried rosemary
1 tsp. (5 mL) dried thyme
$\frac{1}{2}$ tsp. (2.5 mL) dried marjoram
$\frac{1}{2}$ tsp. (2.5 mL) salt
dash of ground pepper

Preheat the oven to 375°F (190°C). Mix all the ingredients together in a bowl. Spread them out on a baking sheet and bake for 50 minutes, or until potatoes are tender. If you prefer your vegetables less roasted/more juicy, cover them with foil for the first half of the cooking time.

variation:

Alternately, bake the vegetables in individual parchment packages. First, cut four 12 in. (30 cm) square pieces of baking parchment. Fold each piece in half, then cut each into a half-heart shape and open. Place $\frac{1}{4}$ of the vegetables on each parchment heart, just to one side of the crease. Include fresh sprigs of thyme or rosemary if you have any. Fold the other half of the parchment over again, and make small overlapping folds to seal the edges, starting at the top of the heart. Two in. (5 cm) from the end, twist parchment twice to seal. Bake as above (omitting foil).

sweet potato bake

This rich-tasting side dish is a colorful addition to a special occasion fall or winter meal. (Serves 6–8)

> 6 large sweet potatoes, scrubbed but unpeeled
> ¼ cup (60 mL) margarine
> ¼ cup (60 mL) orange juice
> salt and pepper to taste
> ¼ cup (60 mL) walnut pieces

Preheat the oven to 350°F (175°C). Bake the potatoes until tender. Scoop out the insides and mash thoroughly. Add the orange juice, margarine, and salt and pepper to taste. Combine well. Place in a baking dish and decorate with walnuts. Bake uncovered for 20 minutes.

chinese-style eggplant

This is a yummy side dish, even for eggplant disparagers. Leftovers are delicious cold or added to a pasta dish. (Serves 4)

1 large eggplant, cut into $\frac{1}{2}$ in. (1.2 cm) slices
salt
1 Tbsp. (15 mL) margarine
2 cloves garlic, minced
2 Tbsp. (30 mL) tamari
1 Tbsp. (15 mL) rice vinegar
2 tsp. (10 mL) toasted (dark) sesame oil
$\frac{1}{2}$ tsp. (2.5 mL) sugar
ground black pepper to taste
1 Tbsp. (15 mL) chives, chopped, for garnish

Sprinkle the eggplant slices with salt and let them sit in a colander for 30 minutes. Rinse them and pat dry. In a small frying pan, melt the margarine over medium-low heat. Add the garlic and sauté lightly. Add the tamari, rice vinegar, sesame oil, sugar, and pepper. Cook for 1 minute, then remove from heat. Spread the mixture in a large baking pan. Place the eggplant slices in a single layer in the pan, turning to coat both sides with marinade. Let sit for 30 minutes. Then cook the eggplant under the broiler, a few minutes on each side, until lightly browned. Serve immediately, garnished with chives.

indian-style zucchini with roasted peanuts

*Thank you to Anjani V. Swaminathan for this delicious and filling dish.
In India they use a native gourd, but our garden-variety zucchinis
work just fine. (Serves 6)*

1 Tbsp. (15 mL) vegetable oil

1 ½ tsp. (7.5 mL) mustard seeds

1 ½ tsp (7.5 mL) cumin seeds

1 tsp. (5 mL) chili powder

½ tsp. (2.5 mL) turmeric

6 cups (1.5 L) zucchini, chopped into large bite-sized pieces

2 onions, chopped

1 cup (240 mL) roasted peanuts, chopped fine, but not to a paste

2 tsp. (10 mL) fresh ginger, grated

2 cloves garlic, minced

1 ½ tsp. (7.5 mL) Sambar powder (see Glossary of Ingredients)

1 tsp. (5 mL) salt

In a large saucepan, over medium heat, heat the oil and mustard
seeds until the seeds start to pop. Add the cumin seeds and brown
lightly. Turn the heat to medium-low. Add the chili powder and
turmeric and stir, cooking, for another minute or so. Then add the
zucchini. Stir to coat the zucchini with the oil and spice mixture.
Then cover the pot and simmer, stirring occasionally, until the zucchini is tender, but not mushy (approx. 20 minutes). While the
zucchini is cooking, combine the onions, peanuts, ginger, garlic,
Sambar powder, and salt in a bowl. Mix well and let sit at least
15 minutes. Add the onion mixture to the zucchini. Mix well. Cover
and simmer for an additional 10 minutes. Serve warm.

sautéed greens with portobello mushrooms

These cooked greens provide a welcome alternative to the standard green salad and there are several ways to dress them up. Sauté them with lots of garlic (or garlic plus red pepper flakes, grated ginger, or cumin seed). Splash with tamari just before serving, and top with toasted pine nuts or almonds. (Serves 4)

2 large portobello mushrooms

2 Tbsp. (30 mL) tamari

1½ Tbsp. (22.5 mL) vegan Worcestershire sauce

1½ Tbsp. (22.5 mL) apple cider vinegar

2 tsp. (10 mL) Dijon mustard

2 tsp. (10 mL) toasted (dark) sesame oil

1 Tbsp. (15 mL) olive oil

6 cups (1.5 L) greens (collard, bok choy, beet, swiss chard, spinach), roughly chopped

4 cloves garlic, crushed or minced

salt and pepper to taste

To prepare the mushrooms: remove and discard the stems, wash the caps, and pat them dry with paper towel. In a shallow dish, combine tamari, Worcestershire sauce, cider vinegar, mustard, and sesame oil. Marinate the mushrooms in this mixture for 30 minutes, spooning the marinade over the mushrooms regularly. About 10 minutes before serving time, heat the olive oil in a deep, covered frying pan over medium heat. Add the mushrooms and cook a few minutes on each side, until tender and slightly browned. Reserve the marinade. Remove the mushrooms and set aside. Return the pan to heat. Add the greens, garlic, and reserved marinade and simmer for a few minutes over medium-low heat until greens are tender. Add salt and pepper to taste. Transfer greens to a serving dish. Slice the mushrooms in ½ in. (1.2 cm) slices and arrange on top of the greens.

(Adapted from a recipe that appeared in Vegetarian Times, *Dec. 1998.)*

kale with mustard-tahini sauce

A calcium one-two punch, as kale and tahini are both excellent sources of this important mineral. (Serves 4)

1½ Tbsp. (22.5 mL) olive oil

1 large onion, sliced thinly

8 cups (2 L) kale, sliced thinly across the spine, coarse stem
   ends discarded

1½ cups (360 mL) water

SAUCE:

3 Tbsp. (45 mL) water

2½ Tbsp. (37.5 mL) tahini

1½ Tbsp. (22.5 mL) lemon juice

1 Tbsp. (15 mL) Dijon mustard

¼ tsp. (1.2 mL) salt

In a very large saucepan (with cover), heat the oil over low to medium heat. Sauté the onions until soft. Add the kale and water, stirring to combine. Raise the heat to medium, cover the pot, and cook the kale until tender, about 20 minutes. Combine all the sauce ingredients in a food processor and blend until smooth. Add additional water if the consistency is too thick. When the kale is cooked, drain the excess water. Serve with the sauce dolloped overtop.

savoy cabbage and onion sauté

Comfort food for a long winter evening. Heap this savoy cabbage on a plate with some mashed potatoes, and park yourself in front of a good British TV mystery. (Serves 4)

1 $\frac{1}{2}$ Tbsp. (22.5 mL) olive oil
8 large leaves savoy cabbage, sliced into thin strips across the spine
1 large onion, sliced thinly
1 Tbsp. (15 mL) white vinegar
1 $\frac{1}{2}$ tsp. (7.5 mL) sugar
$\frac{3}{4}$ tsp. (3.75 mL) salt
dash of pepper

Heat the oil in a saucepan over medium heat. Add the onion and cabbage, stirring to coat with oil. Cover and let cook for 15 minutes over low to medium heat, stirring occasionally. Combine the vinegar, sugar, salt, and pepper in a small bowl. Toss with the cooked cabbage and serve.

(Adapted from Edna Staebler's Food That Really Schmecks.*)*

bavarian red cabbage

This tangy side dish is another candidate for a special occasion fall or winter dinner. Its color is outstanding. (Serves 6—8)

2 Tbsp. (30 mL) oil
2 tart red apples, peeled and sliced
1 medium red cabbage (8 cups/2 L), coarsely shredded
$\frac{1}{4}$ cup (60 mL) water
2 Tbsp. (30 mL) brown sugar
2 Tbsp. (30 mL) red wine vinegar
1 bay leaf
1 tsp. (5 mL) salt
pepper to taste

Heat the oil in a large saucepan over medium heat. Cook the apples, stirring, for 3 minutes. Add the remaining ingredients. Stir well. Bring to a boil. Reduce the heat to low and simmer for 35—40 minutes (until cabbage is tender). Remove the bay leaf, add salt and pepper, and serve.

brussels sprouts with pimento and olives

This dish has a slightly smoky, rich flavor. It's a wonderful way to tame the robust flavor of Brussels sprouts. (Serves 6)

4 cups (950 mL) Brussels sprouts, trimmed and halved lengthwise
1 Tbsp. (15 mL) olive oil
1 Tbsp. (15 mL) flour
$\frac{1}{2}$ cup (120 mL) vegetable stock
2 tsp. (10 mL) brown sugar
1$\frac{1}{2}$ tsp. (7.5 mL) dried oregano
$\frac{1}{2}$ tsp. (2.5 mL) dried basil
$\frac{1}{4}$ cup (60 mL) pimento or roasted red pepper strips
6 large black olives, pitted and sliced into rounds

Steam the Brussels sprouts until they're just tender. Set them aside (keeping them warm, if possible). To make the sauce, heat the oil in a small saucepan. Whisk in the flour to form a smooth paste. Then whisk in the stock, brown sugar, oregano, and basil. Cook, stirring frequently, until the sauce thickens. Stir in the red pepper and olives. Reheat the Brussels sprouts if necessary. Pour the sauce over the Brussels sprouts and serve.

stuffed grapevine leaves

Once you get the hang of rolling up the leaves, these are easy and fun to make. (You know, one of those soothing, meditative activities…) Stuffed grapevine leaves are highly versatile—great for lunches, picnics, and snacks. (Makes 25–30)

2 Tbsp. (30 mL) olive oil
1 onion, minced
1 stalk celery, minced
1 carrot, minced
2 cloves garlic, minced
2½ cups (600 mL) cooked brown rice
1 14 oz. (398 mL) can crushed tomatoes
2 tsp. (10 mL) ground cumin
2 tsp. (10 mL) dried mint
juice of 1 lemon
salt and pepper to taste
1 16 oz. (475 mL) jar of preserved grapevine leaves, drained and rinsed

To prepare the filling: Heat the oil in a large frying pan over medium heat. Sauté the onion, celery, carrot, and garlic until soft. Combine with the rice, tomatoes, cumin, mint, lemon juice, and salt and pepper in a large bowl.

To stuff the grapevine leaves: Place one leaf down flat, stem-end toward you. Place approximately 1 Tbsp. (15 mL) of filling near the base, and roll tightly, folding in the sides as you go. Place on a lightly oiled baking sheet. Repeat until the filling is used up. Preheat the oven to 350°F (175°C). Drizzle the rolls with additional olive oil if desired. Bake for 20–25 minutes. Serve warm or cold.

quinoa pilaff with apricots and currants

Quinoa (pronounced keen-wa)—grain of the Aztecs—is an excellent source of protein. You can experiment with this pilaff in a variety of ways: add additional vegetables to the onion sauté, vary the herbs, or stir in toasted nuts or seeds after the quinoa has finished cooking. This pilaff also works well with bulgur, which can be substituted directly for the quinoa. (Serves 4)

1 Tbsp. (15 mL) olive oil

1 onion, minced

1 cup (240 mL) quinoa, rinsed thoroughly

2 cups (475 mL) vegetable stock

$1/_4$ cup (60 mL) currants

$1/_4$ cup (60 mL) apricots, diced

$1/_4$ cup (60 mL) fresh parsley, minced

salt and pepper to taste

Heat the oil in a large saucepan. Sauté the onion over medium heat until soft. Stir in the quinoa and cook, stirring, for 1 minute. Stir in the stock, currants, and apricots. Bring to a boil, reduce heat, cover and simmer slowly until liquid is absorbed, about 20 minutes. Stir in the parsley. Season with salt and pepper to taste.

barley-mushroom pilaff

Mushroom and barley is a classic combination, and it works to good effect in this recipe. Pot barley is the whole grain, and takes longer to cook than the more processed pearl barley (which is less nutritious). Because of the long cooking time, I only make this dish when I'm going to have the oven on anyway, for baking, etc. (Serves 3–4)

  1 ½ cups (360 mL) mushrooms, sliced
  2 Tbsp. (30 mL) olive oil
  1 onion, sliced thinly
  ¾ cup (180 mL) pot barley
  1 tsp. (5 mL) dried dill
  3 cups (720 mL) hot vegetable broth
  salt and pepper to taste

Preheat the oven to 350°F (175°C). In a medium saucepan, sauté the mushrooms in 1 Tbsp. (15 mL) olive oil until tender. Lift them out with a slotted spoon. In the same pan, add the onions and remaining olive oil. Sauté onions for about 5 minutes, until golden. Add the barley and cook over low heat, stirring frequently, until it is slightly browned, about 5 minutes. Remove the barley from heat. Stir in the mushrooms, dill, and 1 cup (240 mL) broth. Turn the mixture into a 1 quart (1 L) baking dish, and bake, covered, for 30 minutes. Stir in another cup (240 mL) of vegetable broth. Cover and bake 30 minutes longer. Finally, stir in the remaining broth and bake 20 minutes longer. Season with salt and pepper to taste.

lime rice

Thank you to Arpita Anant for sharing this delightfully refreshing South Indian recipe. It's a perfect make-ahead summer dish. (Serves 4)

2 cups (475 mL) water
1 cup (240 mL) white basmati rice
3 Tbsp. (45 mL) fresh lime juice
$^1/_4$ cup (60 mL) fresh cilantro, minced
2 tsp. (10 mL) fresh ginger, grated
$^1/_2$ tsp. (2.5 mL) salt
2 Tbsp. (30 mL) vegetable oil
1 tsp. (5 mL) mustard seeds
2 tsp. (10 mL) cumin seeds
1 jalapeno pepper, seeded and sliced thinly
$^1/_2$ tsp. (2.5 mL) turmeric
$^1/_4$ tsp. (1.2 mL) asafoetida (optional)

In a medium, covered saucepan, bring the rice and water to boil. Reduce the heat to low and simmer for 20 minutes, or until rice is cooked. Remove from heat and cool completely, and then transfer to a serving dish. Add the lime juice, cilantro, ginger, and salt to the cooled rice, and combine gently. Heat the oil and mustard seeds in a small, thick-bottomed saucepan over medium heat until the seeds start to pop. Add the cumin seeds and brown lightly. Turn the heat down to low. Add the jalapeno pepper, turmeric, and asafoetida and continue to cook until the pepper softens (5 to 10 minutes). Remove from heat and stir into the rice mixture. Serve at room temperature.

main dishes

sweet and sour lentils

A quick and yummy way to prepare lentils. Serve with rice or a baked potato. (Serves 4)

1 cup (240 mL) green or brown lentils
2 cups (475 mL) vegetable stock
1 bay leaf
$\frac{1}{4}$ cup (60 mL) brown sugar
$\frac{1}{4}$ cup (60 mL) apple or pineapple juice
$\frac{1}{4}$ cup (60 mL) cider vinegar
1 clove garlic, minced
$\frac{1}{8}$ tsp. (.5 mL) ground cloves
salt to taste

Combine the stock, lentils, and bay leaf in a medium saucepan. Bring to a boil, then simmer, covered, until lentils are cooked (approximately 30 minutes). Add the remaining ingredients. Heat thoroughly and serve.

variation:
For curried lentils, cook the lentils as per first step above. Then sauté 1 large onion, chopped, and 1 clove garlic, minced, in 2 Tbsp. (30 mL) olive oil. Add 1–2 Tbsp. (15–30 mL) curry powder. Fry briefly. Add to cooked lentils with 2 Tbsp. (30 mL) lemon juice, 2 Tbsp. (30 mL) chopped parsley, and salt to taste.

squash and lentil stew with sage

Make this great late fall stew just before your herb garden is buried in snow. The combination of earthy sage and smoky veggie bacon is irresistible. (Serves 4)

1 small butternut squash
1 Tbsp. (15 mL) olive oil
1 large onion, chopped
1 Tbsp. (15 mL) veggie bacon bits
$\frac{2}{3}$ cup (160 mL) green or brown lentils
1 $\frac{1}{2}$ cups (360 mL) vegetable stock
20 leaves fresh sage (approx.)
salt and pepper to taste

Cut the squash in half, and scoop out the seeds. Then peel the squash and cut into bite-sized pieces. Heat the oil in a medium pot over medium heat. Sauté the onion and veggie bacon until onion is soft. Add the lentils, vegetable stock, and sage leaves. Cover and simmer for about 15 minutes. Add the squash and continue to simmer until the squash and lentils are cooked (approx. 20 minutes more). Season with salt and pepper to taste.

tarragon lentil-nut loaf

I make this versatile, delicious, and filling loaf once per week in winter, and almost as often in the summer. The first night I serve it hot, usually with a sauce. The herb flavor is even better the second day, so leftovers are great served cold or in a sandwich. (Serves 6)

1 cup (240 mL) green lentils
2 cups (475 mL) vegetable stock
1 bay leaf
1 large onion, roughly chopped
1 $\frac{1}{2}$ cups (360 mL) mushrooms
2 Tbsp. (30 mL) olive oil
1 cup (240 mL) walnuts
1 cup (240 mL) fine bread crumbs
$\frac{1}{4}$ cup (60 mL) packed fresh tarragon (sage is also very nice), or
    2 Tbsp. (30 mL) dried
1 $\frac{1}{2}$ Tbsp. (22.5 mL) rice vinegar
1 Tbsp. (15 mL) tamari
1 tsp. (5 mL) salt

Preheat the oven to 350°F (175°C). Combine the lentils, stock, and bay leaf in a small saucepan. Bring to a boil, then turn down and simmer, covered, until lentils are soft (approximately $\frac{1}{2}$ hour). Mince the onion and mushrooms in a food processor. Heat the oil in a large frying pan, and sauté mushrooms and onion until soft. Mince the walnuts, bread crumbs, and herbs in food processor. Add to the onion/mushroom mixture along with the vinegar, tamari, salt, and cooked lentils. Mix well. Turn ingredients into an oiled (or sprayed) loaf pan. Bake for

35—40 minutes. Loosen the sides and turn the loaf out onto a serving plate. Decorate it with sprigs of tarragon or other herbs.

variation:

This can be served plain or with a sauce. The Hungarian Mushroom Soup (p. 52) can be adapted to make a great sauce by reducing the stock to 1 cup (240 mL) total. Moroccan Tomato Sauce (p. 113) also works well. Or simply melt a bit of red currant jelly and drizzle overtop.

(Adapted from The Toronto Humane Society's Vegetarian Cookbook.)

beans 'n' greens

*Serve these quick 'n' delicious beans on a bed of mashed potatoes.
(Or even better, on a bed of mashed potatoes spiked with steamed
carrots and green beans, finely chopped fresh savory and sage, and a
dollop of soy yogurt.) (Serves 2—3)*

> 6—8 cloves garlic, minced
> 1 Tbsp. (15 mL) olive oil
> 10 sage leaves, minced
> 1 19 oz. (532 mL) can white kidney beans, rinsed and drained
> 2 cups (475 mL) vegetable stock
> 4 cups (950 mL) packed fresh greens (spinach, chard, beet greens,
>   arugula, or collards)
> salt to taste

In a large pan, sauté the garlic in oil over low to medium heat for
2 minutes. Add the sage and continue to sauté for a minute. Add the
beans and stir. Add 1 cup (240 mL) vegetable stock, and simmer the
beans over medium heat until the liquid is absorbed. Add the remaining stock and simmer until it's half-absorbed. Add the greens and
simmer until cooked (approx. 5 minutes). Add salt to taste.

maple baked beans

We can only hope that the pioneers' lives were made a little easier by such pleasing fare. (Serves 4–6)

1²⁄₃ cups (400 mL) uncooked navy beans (or 4 cups/950 mL cooked)
1 6 oz. (170 mL) can tomato paste
½ cup (120 mL) maple syrup
2½ Tbsp. (37.5 mL) tamari
2 tsp. (10 mL) paprika
½ tsp. (2.5 mL) dry mustard
pinch cayenne

If you're using uncooked beans, place them in a medium saucepan and cover them generously with water. Bring to a boil, cover, and boil them gently for 2 minutes. Turn off the heat and let them stand for 1 hour. Drain the beans and cover them generously with fresh water. Simmer until the beans are cooked (approximately 1 hour). Preheat the oven to 350°F (175°C). Drain the cooked beans and combine them with remaining ingredients in a small casserole dish. Bake, uncovered, for 40 minutes.

black-eyed beans with cumin

Cooking the cumin seed and cinnamon in oil before adding the other ingredients is crucial, as this fully releases their flavor. (Serves 4–6)

1 ⅓ cups (320 mL) uncooked black-eyed beans
3 Tbsp. (45 mL) vegetable oil
2 Tbsp. (30 mL) cumin seeds
1 in. (2.5 cm) cinnamon bark
2 medium onions, chopped
4 cloves garlic, minced
3 cups (720 mL) white mushrooms, sliced
1 14 oz. (398 mL) can diced tomatoes
2 tsp. (10 mL) coriander
1 tsp. (5 mL) cumin
½ tsp. (2.5 mL) turmeric
½ tsp. (2.5 mL) cayenne
2 tsp. (10 mL) salt
pepper to taste
¼ cup (60 mL) fresh cilantro (or parsley), chopped, for garnish

Place the beans in a medium saucepan and cover generously with water. Bring to a boil, cover, and boil gently for 2 minutes. Turn off the heat and let stand for 1 hour. Drain the beans and cover generously with fresh water. Simmer until beans are cooked (approximately 1 hour). Drain the cooked beans, retaining 1 cup (240 mL) of broth. Heat the oil in a large frying pan over medium-low heat. Add the cumin seeds and cinnamon. Brown the spices, but be careful not to burn them. Add the onions and garlic and brown lightly. Add the mushrooms and sauté until wilted. Add the tomatoes, coriander, cumin, turmeric, and cayenne. Simmer for 10 minutes. Add the beans and reserved broth. Heat through. Add the salt, pepper, and cilantro.

(Adapted from Madhur Jaffrey's World-of-the-East Vegetarian Cooking.*)*

tangy black beans à l'orange

I like to make this bean dish for company. The zesty flavor and black and orange contrasts make for an exotic presentation. (Serves 4)

1 Tbsp. (15 mL) olive oil
1 large onion, chopped
1 red bell pepper, seeded and chopped
2 cloves garlic, minced
1 cup (240 mL) black beans, uncooked
3 cups (720 mL) vegetable stock
1 bay leaf
1 tsp. (5 mL) white vinegar
1 14 oz. (398 mL) can diced tomatoes
1 orange, washed and sliced in half
2 stalks celery, chopped
1 carrot, peeled and chopped
1 sweet potato, peeled and diced
salt to taste

Heat the oil in a large pot over medium heat. Sauté the onion, pepper, and garlic until soft. Add the beans, stock, bay leaf, and vinegar. Bring to a boil, then reduce heat and simmer for 2 minutes. Take off the stove and let sit, covered, for 1 hour. Add the remaining ingredients and simmer on low, with lid ajar, for 2—3 hours more, until beans are tender. Remove a ladleful of beans, mash them, and return them to the pot to thicken the mixture.

(Adapted from Frances Moore Lappé's Diet for a Small Planet.*)*

spicy chickpea curry

A wonderful combination of spices that explode in the mouth without being unduly hot. To vary this recipe, replace the chickpeas with grilled eggplant (one large or 6 small Italian eggplants). (Serves 4—6)

3 Tbsp. (45 mL) vegetable oil
1 tsp. (5 mL) fennel seeds
$\frac{1}{2}$ tsp. (2.5 mL) mustard seeds
1 28 oz. (796 mL) can diced tomatoes
$1\frac{1}{2}$ Tbsp. (22.5 mL) fresh ginger, grated
4 cloves garlic, minced
$1\frac{1}{2}$ Tbsp. (22.5 mL) coriander
2 tsp. (10 mL) ground cumin
1 tsp. (5 mL) cayenne
$\frac{1}{2}$ tsp. (2.5 mL) turmeric
$1\frac{1}{2}$ tsp. (7.5 mL) salt
2 19 oz. (532 mL) cans chickpeas, rinsed and drained

Heat the oil in a large frying pan. Add the fennel and mustard seeds. Cook for a few minutes over medium heat, being careful not to burn them. When they pop, add the tomatoes, ginger, garlic, and other spices. Cook, stirring, until the mixture thickens slightly. Add the chickpeas and cover. Simmer on medium-low for 10 minutes.

chili sensation

If you're feeding a crowd, chili is an easy, informal way to go. Serve with a giant salad and lots of good bread. (Serves 6—8)

2 Tbsp. (30 mL) olive oil

2 large onions, sliced thinly

1 8$\frac{1}{2}$ oz. (240 g) package tempeh, thawed (or substitute "veggie ground round")

1 medium carrot, peeled and chopped

1 red or green bell pepper, seeded and chopped

1 28 oz. (796 mL) can crushed tomatoes

2 fresh tomatoes, chopped

1 19 oz. (532 mL) can red kidney beans (or black beans, or chickpeas), drained and rinsed

3 Tbsp. (45 mL) chili powder

1 tsp. (5 mL) salt

1 tsp. (5 mL) ground cumin

$\frac{1}{2}$ tsp. (2.5 mL) turmeric

$\frac{1}{2}$ tsp. (2.5 mL) ground coriander

$\frac{1}{8}$ tsp. (.5 mL) cinnamon

$\frac{1}{8}$ tsp. (.5 mL) ground cloves

pinch of cayenne

$\frac{1}{2}$ cup (120 mL) fresh cilantro, roughly chopped

Heat the oil in a large saucepan over medium heat. Sauté the onions until soft. Crumble the tempeh into tiny pieces and add it to the onion. Continue cooking over medium heat for a few minutes, stirring regularly. Then add the carrot and pepper and continue to sauté 2—3 minutes longer. Add the remaining ingredients, except cilantro, and simmer for 1 hour. Garnish with cilantro.

curried rice and tempeh salad

This recipe isn't as difficult as it looks. In any case, it's worth the effort. The inclusion of tempeh makes it hearty enough to serve as a main course. It's also an excellent buffet salad. The salad consists of 4 components: rice, tempeh, vegetables, and dressing. (Serves 6)

RICE:

2 whole cloves

$1/2$ tsp. (2.5 mL) each: cumin seeds, turmeric, coriander seeds or powder, chili powder

$1/4$ tsp. (1.2 mL) each: ground cardamom, cinnamon, cayenne

$1/8$ tsp. (.5 mL) fennel seeds

$1/2$ Tbsp. (7.5 mL) oil

$1/2$ tsp. (2.5 mL) mustard seeds

3 cloves garlic, minced

1 Tbsp. (15 mL) fresh ginger, grated

1 cup (240 mL) brown basmati rice, rinsed

$1 3/4$ cups (420 mL) water

1 tsp. (5 mL) salt

TEMPEH:

1 $8 1/2$ oz. (240 g) package tempeh, thawed

1 Tbsp. (15 mL) olive oil

$1/2$ cup (120 mL) vegetable stock

1 Tbsp. (15 mL) tamari

VEGETABLES:

1 large carrot, peeled and diced

1 cup (240 mL) frozen peas or fresh snow peas

1 red bell pepper, seeded and chopped

3 green onions, finely chopped

$1/4$ cup (60 mL) currants

2 Tbsp. (30 mL) lemon juice

2 Tbsp. (30 mL) cider vinegar

$\frac{1}{2}$ tsp. (2.5 mL) salt

2 Tbsp. (30 mL) olive oil

To prepare the rice: With a mortar and pestle or spice grinder, pulverize the dry spices except for the mustard seeds. Heat the oil in a medium saucepan over low heat. Add the mustard seeds. When they begin to pop, add the garlic and ginger and sauté briefly. Stir in the pulverized spice mixture and cook, stirring constantly, for 1 or 2 minutes. Stir in the rice and sauté briefly. Add the water and salt. Bring to a boil, stir once, cover, and reduce heat to low. Cook 40 minutes. Remove from heat, keep covered, and set aside to cool.

To prepare the tempeh: Use a sharp knife to cut it in half, then cut each half into 2 thin layers. Heat the oil in a large frying pan over medium heat. Brown the tempeh on both sides. Reduce the heat to low. Add the stock, cover tightly, and steam the tempeh until liquid is almost absorbed. Add the tamari and cook until the pan is dry. Cut the tempeh into bite-sized strips.

To prepare the vegetables: Lightly steam or sauté the carrots and peas until tender-crisp. Combine with other vegetables.

To prepare the dressing: Whisk together the lemon juice, vinegar, and salt. Gradually whisk in the oil.

To assemble the salad: In a large bowl, toss together the cooled rice, tempeh, and vegetables. Drizzle the dressing overtop and fold it in thoroughly. Let it sit for at least 1 hour for flavors to develop. Serve the salad on a bed of torn greens, if desired, garnished with toasted almonds or cashews, or lightly toasted, flaked, unsweetened coconut.

(Adapted from a recipe that appeared in Vegetarian Times, *Nov. 1992)*

indonesian-style tempeh and coconut curry

This is a decadent, creamy dish. Best served with plain rice and a green salad, or a simple stir-fry of julienned carrots and snow peas. (Serves 4)

1 small head broccoli, cut into bite-sized pieces
1 8½ oz. (240 g) package tempeh, thawed
2 Tbsp. (30 mL) olive oil
½ cup (120 mL) green onions, chopped
1 clove garlic, minced
1 jalapeno pepper, seeded and minced
1 Tbsp. (15 mL) fresh ginger, minced
1 14 oz. (398 mL) can coconut milk
1 Tbsp. (15 mL) Patak's mild curry paste
¾ tsp. (4 mL) salt

Steam the broccoli until tender-crisp, then plunge it into cold water and set aside to drain. Cut the tempeh in half. Using a sharp knife, cut each piece into 2 thin layers. Heat 1 Tbsp. (15 mL) oil in a large frying pan over medium heat. Add the tempeh and brown on both sides. Remove the tempeh from the pan and cut it into bite-sized pieces. Set aside. Return the pan to low to medium heat and add the remaining 1 Tbsp. (15 mL) oil. Add the green onions and garlic and cook for 1 minute. Add the jalapeno pepper and ginger and cook for 1 minute longer. Add the coconut milk, curry paste, salt, and tempeh pieces. Simmer gently, covered, for 10 minutes. Add the steamed broccoli pieces and heat through. Serve immediately.

tempeh and snow pea stir-fry

A quick and delicious meal (as long as you remembered to defrost the tempeh!). Serve with rice. (Serves 3—4)

1 8½ oz. (240 g) package tempeh, thawed
2 Tbsp. (30 mL) olive oil
1½ cups (360 mL) carrots, peeled and sliced into thin rounds
5 cloves garlic, minced
¾ cup (180 mL) vegetable stock
1½ cups (360 mL) snow peas
1 red onion, thinly sliced
1 Tbsp. (15 mL) tamari
2 Tbsp. (30 mL) rice vinegar
2 Tbsp. (30 mL) sugar
1 tsp. (5 mL) salt

Cut the tempeh in half. Using a sharp knife, cut each piece into 2 thin layers. Heat 1 Tbsp. (15 mL) oil in a large frying pan over medium heat. Add the tempeh and brown on both sides. Remove from heat. Cut the tempeh into bite-sized strips and set aside. Return the pan to medium heat. Add the remaining 1 Tbsp. (15 mL) oil. Add the carrot rounds and garlic and sauté briefly. Add the stock and simmer, stirring occasionally, until carrots are tender (a couple of minutes). Add the snow peas, onion, tamari, vinegar, sugar, salt, and tempeh pieces. Toss well and cook over medium-high heat for about 2 minutes.

moroccan-style tempeh with apricots, dates, and olives

A rich and satisfying alternative to the traditional Moroccan meat-based dish cooked in a tagine (a shallow earthenware dish with a conical lid). Serve on a bed of couscous, with a simple green salad accompaniment. (Serves 4)

1 8½ oz. (240 g) package tempeh, thawed

2 Tbsp. (30 mL) olive oil

1 large onion, thinly sliced

2 cloves garlic, minced

2 bay leaves

2 tsp. (10 mL) turmeric

2 tsp. (10 mL) ground cardamom

2 tsp. (10 mL) ground coriander

2 cinnamon sticks, broken in large pieces

1 cup (240 mL) dry white wine

2½ cups (600 mL) vegetable stock

½ cup (120 mL) mixed green and black olives, pitted and
   roughly chopped

½ cup (120 mL) dried apricots, quartered

¼ cup (60 mL) currants

4 large dried dates, pitted and quartered

2 Tbsp. (30 mL) capers, drained

salt and pepper to taste

Preheat the oven to 350°F (175°F). Cut the tempeh in half. Using a sharp knife, cut each piece into 2 thin layers. Heat 1 Tbsp. (15 mL) oil in a large frying pan over medium heat. Add the tempeh and brown on both sides. Remove from the pan and cut it into bite-sized pieces. Set aside. Return the pan to low to medium heat. Add the remaining 1 Tbsp. (15 mL) oil. Sauté the onion and garlic until soft. Add the bay leaves, turmeric, cardamom, coriander, and cinnamon sticks. Cook slowly for 4—5 minutes, stirring occasionally, to allow spices to release their flavor. Add the wine and cook for 3—4 minutes, to let the alcohol evaporate. Add the stock, olives, apricots, currants, dates, and capers. Stir well. Bring to a boil. Add the tempeh pieces and stir well. Remove from heat and turn into a medium-sized, covered casserole. Bake for 45 minutes. Season to taste.

———————————

To make couscous: Bring 1½ cups (360 mL) water to the boil in a medium saucepan. Add 1½ cups (360 mL) couscous. When water returns to the boil, remove pan from heat, cover, and let sit for 5 minutes. Fluff the couscous with a fork and it's ready to serve.

(Adapted from a recipe by Merla McMenomy in The Globe and Mail*)*

tempeh stroganoff

This isn't really a separate recipe, just a clever combination that's sure to satisfy anyone who's hungering for a rich and "meaty" dish. (Serves 4)

> 1 batch of Hungarian Mushroom Sauce (p. 52). Note that to make sauce instead of soup you use 1 cup (240 mL) stock in total.
> 1 Tbsp. (15 mL) olive oil
> 1 8½ oz. (240 g) package tempeh, thawed
> ½ cup (120 mL) vegetable stock
> 1 Tbsp. (15 mL) tamari

Prepare the mushroom sauce and set it aside. Cut the tempeh in half. Using a sharp knife, cut each piece into 2 thin layers. Heat the oil over medium heat in a large frying pan. Brown the tempeh on both sides. Add the stock and tamari. Cover tightly and steam the tempeh until liquid is almost absorbed. Remove the tempeh and cut it into bite-sized strips. Return it to the pan. Add the mushroom sauce and reheat gently. Serve over rice or noodles.

winter ragout

Delicious served with bread and a salad or on a bed of mashed potatoes with cooked green peas. (Instead of the usual margarine and salt, try finishing peas with salt, pepper, a splash of toasted sesame oil, and a sprinkling of toasted sesame seeds.) (Serves 6)

3 Tbsp. (45 mL) olive oil

3 stalks celery, finely chopped

2 large onions, finely chopped

3$\frac{1}{2}$ cups (840 mL) vegetable stock

1 8$\frac{1}{2}$ oz. (240 g) package tempeh, thawed and cut into small, bite-sized pieces

1 6 oz. (170 mL) can tomato paste

$\frac{1}{2}$ cup (120 mL) red wine

2 medium potatoes, chopped in bite-sized pieces (or substitute sweet potatoes, squash, or turnip)

4 medium carrots, peeled and chopped in bite-sized pieces

1 fennel bulb (top and base removed), cut into $\frac{1}{2}$ in. (1.2 cm) wedges

2 cups (475 mL) mushrooms, quartered

2 cups (475 mL) pearl onions, peeled

6 cloves garlic, peeled and smashed

1$\frac{1}{2}$ Tbsp. (22.5 mL) tamari

1$\frac{1}{2}$ Tbsp. (22.5 mL) balsamic vinegar

10 large sage leaves

2 bay leaves

1 tsp. (5 mL) dried thyme

1 tsp. (5 mL) salt

pepper to taste

In a large covered pot, heat oil over medium-low heat. Sauté the celery and onions until very soft and golden. Add remaining ingredients to the pot, and simmer for an hour over medium-low heat, thinning with additional stock if necessary. Add additional salt and pepper to taste.

korean tofu

Sponge-like tofu is an excellent candidate for marinade. This dish looks quite elegant served with plain rice and sautéed vegetables. Leftovers make a delicious cold snack or sandwich filling. (Serves 4)

1 lb. (455 g) medium-firm tofu, drained and cut into $^1/_4$ in. (.6 cm) slices
$^1/_3$ cup (80 mL) tamari
3 Tbsp. (45 mL) sugar
2 cloves garlic, minced
1 $^1/_2$ tsp. (7.5 mL) onion powder
1 tsp. (5 mL) dry mustard
1 Tbsp. (15 mL) vegetable oil
$^1/_4$ cup (60 mL) chives, chopped, for garnish

Place the tofu slices in a single layer in a shallow dish. Combine the tamari, sugar, garlic, onion powder, and mustard in a small bowl. Pour over tofu. Marinate in the fridge for two hours minimum. Then heat the oil in a large frying pan and brown the tofu on both sides. Add any leftover marinade to the pan at the last minute, then remove from heat. Garnish the tofu with chives.

(Adapted from Louise Hagler's Tofu Cookery.)

tofu satay

If you marinate the tofu in the morning, this dish will be ready to pop into the oven when you get home for a quick and delectable meal. Serve with rice and sautéed vegetables such as carrots, zucchini, or snow peas. (Serves 4)

$\frac{1}{2}$ cup (120 mL) boiling water
$\frac{1}{3}$ cup (80 mL) smooth peanut butter
$\frac{1}{3}$ cup (80 mL) tamari
1 $\frac{1}{2}$ Tbsp. (22.5 mL) vegetable oil
1 Tbsp. (15 mL) rice syrup
3 cloves garlic, minced
2 tsp. (10 mL) fresh ginger, grated
1 tsp. (5 mL) white vinegar
$\frac{1}{2}$ tsp. (2.5 mL) salt
dash of cayenne
1 lb. (455 g) medium-firm tofu, drained and cut into $\frac{1}{4}$ in (.6cm) slices

Combine all the ingredients except for the tofu in a food processor and process until smooth. Lightly oil or spray the bottom of a baking dish large enough to accommodate the tofu slices in a single layer. Cover the bottom with a thin layer of the sauce. Then place the tofu slices on top. Pour the remaining sauce overtop. Marinate in the fridge for 2—3 hours minimum. Preheat the oven to 350°F (175°C). Bake for 20—25 minutes.

(Adapted from Louise Hagler's Tofu Cookery.)

the fredericton rice bowl

A meal in a bowl. Meredith Levine created this delicious recipe and named it after her home town, although the inspiration seems more Thailand than New Brunswick... (Serves 4)

SAUCE:

1 14 oz. (398 mL) can coconut milk

1 cup (240 mL) vegetable stock

3 stalks lemongrass, tough parts discarded and tender inner
   leaves unfurled

1 Tbsp. (15 mL) white wine

1 Tbsp. (15 mL) tamari

1 1/2 tsp. (7.5 mL) Thai green curry paste

salt to taste

RICE BASE:

1 Tbsp. (15 mL) vegetable oil

2 ribs celery, diced

1 onion, diced

1 1/2 cups (360 mL) brown basmati rice

3 cups (720 mL) vegetable stock

TOFU AND VEGETABLE TOPPINGS:

1 lb. (455 g) silken tofu, drained

2 carrots, peeled and julienned

1/2 red bell pepper, seeded and cut in thin strips

2 cups (475 mL) packed baby spinach

1 bunch asparagus, steamed and chopped (or substitute steamed
   cauliflower or green beans)

Combine the sauce ingredients in a large deep-sided pan. Simmer over low to medium heat for 1 hour, making vegetable additions as instructed below.

Begin the rice by heating the oil in a medium-sized saucepan. Add the celery and onion and sauté over low to medium heat until soft (about 5 minutes). Add the rice and stir for 1 minute. Add the stock, bring to a boil, cover, reduce heat to low, and simmer until cooked (about 45 minutes).

While the rice is cooking, break the tofu into 4 chunks and add to the simmering sauce. (The silken tofu will gradually fall apart in the sauce, but try to keep some bite-sized chunks if you can.) Then add the carrots and red pepper to the sauce. After the sauce has simmered 55 minutes, and the liquid has reduced by half, remove the strands of lemongrass and discard. Test the sauce for salt. Add the spinach and steamed asparagus to the sauce and heat through.

To serve, divide the rice mixture between 4 large pasta bowls. Spoon sauce, tofu, and vegetables over each portion. Serve with a spoon and fork, as the consistency is quite soupy.

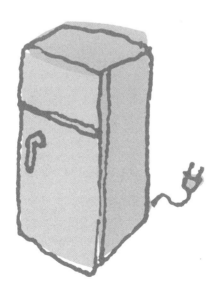

ribollita

A Tuscan classic. Don't stint on the bread—this is real comfort food, thick and mushy. Make it a day ahead as it must spend a night in the fridge before being "re-boiled." (Serves 6—8)

1 Tbsp. (15 mL) olive oil
2 cups (475 mL) shredded red or green cabbage (or a mixture
    of cabbage and kale)
1 large onion, diced
1 zucchini, diced
2 cloves garlic, minced
7 cups (1.75 L) vegetable stock
2 cups (475 mL) potatoes, diced
$1\frac{1}{2}$ Tbsp. (22.5 mL) dried parsley
1 Tbsp. (15 mL) dried oregano
$1\frac{1}{2}$ tsp. (7.5 mL) dried basil
$\frac{1}{2}$ tsp. (2.5 mL) each salt and pepper
1 28 oz. (796 mL) can crushed tomatoes
1 14 oz. (398 mL) can white kidney beans, drained and rinsed
several slices day-old bread

In a large saucepan, heat the oil over medium heat. Add the cabbage, onion, zucchini, and garlic and cook, stirring occasionally, for 5 to 7 minutes. Add the stock, potatoes, herbs, salt, and pepper. Cook for 10 minutes over medium heat. Add the tomatoes and beans and simmer for about 30 minutes, stirring occasionally. Remove from heat and cool. Refrigerate overnight. To serve, reheat the soup and simmer for 10 minutes. Place the torn bread (1 or 2 slices) into the bottom of each soup bowl. Ladle the hot soup over the bread and let it stand for a couple of minutes. Garnish with soy "parmesan" if desired.

(Adapted from a recipe that appeared in Vegetarian Times, *Nov. 1996)*

hearty lentil soup with cloves

Cloves—the viol da gamba *of spices—occupy a niche of their own, adding a unique depth and complexity to any dish.* (Serves 4–6)

3 Tbsp. (45 mL) olive oil
2 onions, sliced thinly
2 carrots, peeled and diced
2 stalks celery, diced
2 cloves garlic, minced
8 cups (2 L) vegetable stock
1 1/2 cups (360 mL) green or brown lentils
1/2 cup (120 mL) tomato paste
15 whole cloves tied in cheesecloth
2 bay leaves
1/4 cup (60 mL) parsley, roughly chopped
1 tsp. (5 mL) dried thyme
2 cups (480 mL) potatoes, diced
1 tsp. (5 mL) paprika
salt and pepper to taste
2 Tbsp. (30 mL) dry sherry (optional)

Heat the oil in a large saucepan over medium heat. Sauté the onions, carrots, celery, and garlic until soft, but not browned. Add the stock, lentils, tomato paste, cloves, bay leaf, parsley, and thyme. Bring to a boil, cover, and simmer at low heat for 1 hour. Add the potatoes, paprika, and salt and pepper to taste, and continue to simmer until the potatoes are soft (about 15 minutes). Just before serving, remove the bay leaves and cloves. Add sherry if desired.

minestrone

As with Hearty Lentil Soup (previous page), cloves are the secret ingredient here, lending a full-bodied flavor. This is so thick it's really a stew. (Serves 4)

2 Tbsp. (30 mL) olive oil

2 onions, chopped

1 carrot, peeled and diced

1 stalk celery, diced

1 cup (240 mL) diced eggplant

1 red bell pepper, seeded and chopped

3 cups (720 mL) vegetable stock

1 28 oz. (796 mL) can crushed tomatoes

1 tsp. (5 mL) dried oregano

1 tsp. (5 mL) dried basil

5 whole cloves tied in a cheesecloth

1 cup (240 mL) dry short pasta like fusilli or penne

1 19 oz. (532 mL) can white kidney beans (or chickpeas, or
   black beans)

salt to taste

Heat the olive oil in a large pan. Sauté the onions, carrot, celery, eggplant, and pepper until soft. Add the stock, tomatoes, and spices. Simmer for 15 minutes. Add the pasta and cook until tender. Add the beans near the end, just to heat through. Remove cloves just before serving.

*Sauté onions first; then discard +
add remaining vegetables to the pan*

kale and sesame spaghetti

Cook the whole meal in one giant pot. This unusual noodle dish is a simple way to incorporate more calcium-rich kale into your diet. (Serves 4)

    12 cups (3 L) kale, cut in thin strips across the spine, tough
        stems discarded
    13 oz. (375 g) spaghetti or other pasta
    $\frac{1}{4}$ cup (60 mL) sesame seeds
    $\frac{1}{4}$ cup (60 mL) tamari
    3 Tbsp. (45 mL) toasted (dark) sesame oil
    1 tsp. (5 mL) salt

Bring a very large pot of water to a boil. Add the spaghetti and cook for 3—4 minutes. Then add the kale to the same pot, stirring to combine it with noodles. Continue cooking until the spaghetti is *al dente*. Meanwhile, place the sesame seeds in a single layer in a frying pan. Toast them over low-medium heat, stirring occasionally, until medium brown. Drain and transfer the spaghetti to a large bowl. Add the sesame seeds, tamari, sesame oil, and salt. Toss gently and serve hot or at room temperature.

(Adapted from a recipe that appeared in Vegetarian Times, *Feb. 1998.)*

spicy garlic pasta

Some of the best pasta sauces are simple, and an oil and garlic sauce is a welcome break from the usual tomato-based sauces. Experiment until you find your own favorite versions. (Serves 4)

13 oz. (375 g) pasta
$\frac{1}{3}$ cup (80 mL) olive oil
12 cloves garlic, minced
$\frac{1}{2}$ tsp. (2.5 mL) hot red pepper flakes

OPTIONAL EXTRAS:
fresh basil or sage leaves
roasted eggplant slices (see p. 58)
roasted red pepper strips (see p. 58)
capers, drained
olives
fresh tomatoes, diced
chopped broccolini or other greens (spinach, chard, arugula, etc.)

Cook the pasta until *al dente*. Drain, reserving $\frac{2}{3}$ cup (160 mL) cooking water. In a small pan, heat the oil over low-medium heat and sauté the garlic for 1 minute, being careful not to burn it. Add the hot red pepper flakes and optional extras, and toss with garlic for another minute. Then combine the garlic mixture with the pasta and the reserved cooking water. Add an additional splash of olive oil if desired, salt and pepper to taste, and serve.

moroccan tomato sauce

A rich, subtle sauce with beautiful color. Not to be restricted to pasta, it's also a great accompaniment to nut loaf, potatoes, or steamed vegetables with rice. (Serves 6—8)

2 Tbsp. (30 mL) olive oil
2 onions, sliced thinly
5 garlic cloves, minced
2 red bell peppers, seeded and chopped
5 large fresh tomatoes, peeled, seeded, and chopped
1 28 oz. (796 mL) can crushed tomatoes
$\frac{1}{4}$ cup (60 mL) tomato paste
2 Tbsp. (30 mL) paprika
1 tsp. (5 mL) saffron threads (optional)
1 tsp. (5 mL) hot red pepper flakes
$\frac{1}{2}$ tsp. (2.5 mL) turmeric
$\frac{1}{2}$ tsp. (2.5 mL) salt
dash of cayenne
$\frac{1}{4}$ cup (60 mL) chopped fresh cilantro for garnish

Heat the oil in a large pot. Sauté the onions and garlic for about 10 minutes, until soft, but not browned. Add the remaining ingredients, except cilantro. Bring to a boil. Reduce heat and simmer on low for 1 $\frac{1}{2}$ hours, stirring occasionally. Garnish with cilantro.

red pepper and lentil pasta sauce

Lentils add an earthy dimension to this hearty sauce. For those winter days when you know you're burning a lot of carbohydrates. (Serves 4)

1 cup (240 mL) water
$\frac{1}{2}$ cup (120 mL) green or brown lentils
1 bay leaf
3 Tbsp. (45 mL) olive oil
2 onions, sliced thinly
2 cloves garlic, diced
1 red bell pepper, seeded and diced
1 14 oz. (398 mL) can tomato sauce
1 6 oz. (170 mL) can tomato paste
$\frac{1}{2}$ cup (120 mL) red wine
salt and pepper to taste
2 cups (475 mL) mushrooms, sliced

Place the water, lentils, and bay leaf in a small saucepan. Bring to a boil and then reduce to simmer, cooking until the lentils are soft (about $\frac{1}{2}$ hour). Set aside. Heat 2 Tbsp. (30 mL) oil in a large saucepan. Sauté the onions and garlic for 5–10 minutes, until soft, but not browned. Add the red pepper, tomato sauce, tomato paste, and red wine. Bring to a boil, and then reduce heat and simmer on low for 45 minutes. If you like a chunky sauce, leave it as is. If you like a smoother sauce, put it through your food processor to reach the desired consistency. Then add the lentils and simmer 15 minutes longer. Season to taste. In a separate small pan, sauté the mushrooms in the remaining 1 Tbsp. (15 mL) olive oil over medium-high heat until browned. Serve the sauce over your favorite pasta, with mushrooms for garnish.

sundried tomato and basil pesto pizza

A to-die-for pizza topping, which doubles as a delicious pasta sauce.
(Serves 4—6)

   2 pizza crusts, preferably thin
   12 sundried tomatoes
   1 ½ cups (360 mL) boiling water (approx.)
   1 cup (240 mL) packed basil leaves
   ½ cup (120 mL) almonds
   6 cloves garlic, peeled
   2 Tbsp. (30 mL) olive oil
   1 tsp. (5 mL) salt
   pizza toppings of choice (e.g. sliced mushrooms and peppers, pitted
       black olives)

Preheat the oven according to instructions on pizza crust package. In
a small bowl, just cover the tomatoes with boiling water and let them
sit for 15 minutes. Remove the tomatoes (reserve the liquid) and
place in a food processor with the basil, almonds, garlic, olive oil,
and salt. Process until well minced, then add enough of the reserved
liquid to make a sauce-like consistency. Spread the sauce over the
pizza crusts. Add desired toppings and bake on a cookie sheet for
10—12 minutes (or according to package directions).

pissaladière

Many thanks to Colin Macleod for sharing this vegan version of the Provençal classic. Here, strips of roasted red pepper provide a more colorful latticework design than the traditional anchovies. Once you've mastered the art of caramelizing onions, you'll want to use them on everything. They make a great appetizer—just spread them on a lightly toasted baguette. (Serves 6)

 2 cups (475 mL) all purpose flour, plus up to ½ cup (120 mL)
    additional flour for kneading
 1 cup (240 mL) whole wheat flour (or cornmeal)
 2 tsp. (10 mL) salt
 1 cup (240 mL) warm water
 1 Tbsp. (15 mL) yeast
 1 Tbsp. (15 mL) sugar
 ⅔ cup (160 mL) olive oil
 8 large onions, sliced thinly
 4—6 cloves garlic, minced
 1 ½ tsp. (7.5 mL) each dried thyme, marjoram, and rosemary
 1 large red bell pepper, roasted, and cut in strips (see p. 58)
 15—20 black kalamata olives, halved and pitted
 ¼ cup (60 mL) pine nuts
 2 Tbsp. (30 mL) capers, drained

Combine the 2 cups (475 mL) all purpose flour, 1 cup (240 mL) whole wheat flour, and 1 tsp. (5 mL) salt in a large bowl. Form a well in the middle of the bowl. In a separate bowl, combine the warm water, yeast, and sugar. Let sit for 5—10 minutes, until foamy. Add ¼ cup (60 mL) olive oil to the activated yeast mixture, then pour the wet ingredients into the well in the dry ingredients. Gently fold dry into wet until well combined, and form the dough into a ball.

Sprinkle the counter with a small amount of additional flour. Knead the dough (massage it firmly, alternately pressing and turning) for about 10 minutes, adding additional flour to your work surface if the dough begins to stick. Coat the dough ball with a small amount of olive oil, and also coat the inside surface of a small bowl. Set the dough in the bowl and cover with a damp tea towel. Set it in a warm, draft-free place for 1½ hours to rise.

Combine the onions, ⅓ cup (80 mL) olive oil, garlic, herbs, and the remaining 1 tsp. (5 mL) salt in a large, deep-sided pan with a lid. Mix well, cover, and simmer over low to medium heat for 45 minutes. Remove the lid. Continue to simmer on medium heat for another 45 minutes, until the onions are sweet and caramel-colored, with a melt-in-your-mouth consistency. The trick is to cook the onions at a high enough heat so that the liquid is gradually evaporated, but not so high that they dry out. (If they do dry out, add extra olive oil.) When the onions are cooked, set aside.

Preheat the oven to 475°F (250°C). Knead the dough briefly. Then roll it out on a lightly floured surface to fit a large, rectangular cookie sheet. Carefully transfer the dough to the pan. Spoon caramelized onions over the entire surface. Cross two strips of roasted pepper to make an X design over the top of the onions at one corner of the pissaladière crust. Continue with a pattern of linked Xs across the entire surface framing a latticework design. Place a couple of olive halves in each X. Sprinkle pine nuts and capers evenly over the entire surface. Bake the pissaladière for 12—15 minutes, until the crust is lightly browned and the toppings are bubbly. Remove from the oven, let sit for 5 minutes, then slice and serve.

 variation:

If you don't feel like making pizza, use the same toppings as a pasta sauce. Combine the caramelized onions, roasted pepper (sliced), pine nuts (lightly toasted), capers, black olives, and a splash of olive oil, and toss with your favorite pasta.

red and white onion tart

This is a yummy, sweet and savory dish, and it looks great too. It retains its shape on the plate, for elegant presentation, and the contrast of white and red onion is striking. (Serves 6)

1 cup (240 mL) all purpose flour (or combined all purpose and whole wheat)
3 Tbsp. (45 mL) sugar
$\frac{1}{2}$ tsp. (2.5 mL) salt
$\frac{1}{3}$ cup (80 mL) vegetable shortening
2 Tbsp. (30 mL) cold water (approx.)
3 large white onions, sliced very thinly
3 Tbsp. (45 mL) olive oil
1 tsp. (5 mL) cumin seeds
1 $\frac{1}{2}$ cups (360 mL) red pearl onions, peeled
$\frac{1}{4}$ cup (60 mL) water
1 Tbsp. (15 mL) margarine or olive oil
2 cups (475 mL) mushrooms, sliced
1 Tbsp. (15 mL) fresh chives, parsley, or tarragon, minced

Preheat the oven to 325°F (165°C). Combine the flour, 1 Tbsp. (15 mL) sugar, and salt in a bowl. Add the shortening, cutting it in with a pastry knife, or two ordinary knives, until shortening is the size of peas. Add the water gradually, combining well. Form the pastry into a ball, and chill in the freezer for 5—10 minutes. Roll it out between two sheets of waxed paper to prevent sticking. Transfer the crust to a pie plate and crimp the edges. Sprinkle a handful of dried peas or beans in the shell to keep it flat, and bake for 25 minutes. Remove from the oven and set aside. (Discard the beans/peas.)

In a large pan, sauté the white onions in 2 Tbsp. (30 mL) olive oil over low-medium heat until completely soft and slightly browned. Add the cumin seeds and cook for a few minutes longer. Remove from heat and set aside. In a small saucepan, combine the pearl onions, the remaining 2 Tbsp. (30 mL) sugar, water, and margarine or oil. Simmer, covered, until the onions soften. Continue to cook, uncovered, until the water is absorbed and the onions caramelize. Spread white onions around the base of the cooked pastry shell. Arrange pearl onions on top in a central circle. Re-heat the pie in the oven for 10 minutes at 325°F/165°C.

Sauté the mushrooms in the remaining 1 Tbsp. (15 mL) olive oil until browned. Mix in the fresh herbs. Spoon this mixture over the onion tart. Slice and serve.

risotto with lemon and tarragon

Risotto is easy to prepare, but you do have to follow the rules. The liquid has to be absorbed a little bit at a time, so don't get impatient and toss it in all at once. Once you've got the hang of it, experiment with endless variations using mushrooms, steamed asparagus, cauliflower, peas, or beans. You can vary the herbs, too. (E.g. cauliflower with rosemary, or peas with mint.) (Serves 4)

 3 Tbsp. (45 mL) olive oil
 3 large leeks, sliced thinly
 1½ cups (360 mL) arborio rice
 ½ cup (120 mL) white wine
 2 Tbsp. (30 mL) fresh tarragon, chopped
 zest of one lemon (plus 1 or 2 lemon wedges if desired)
 4 cups (950 mL) vegetable stock

Heat the oil over medium heat in a large, deep frying pan. Sauté the leeks until soft. Add the rice and cook for a minute or two. Add the wine and continue to cook, stirring regularly, until the liquid is absorbed. Add the tarragon, lemon zest, and 1 cup (240 mL) stock. Continue stirring until the liquid is fully absorbed. Keep the heat at medium-low so the liquid doesn't evaporate too quickly. Continue stirring and adding stock, 1 cup (240 mL) at a time, being sure to let it absorb completely each time. Serve immediately.

roasted vegetable couscous with sundried tomato pesto

A delicious summer dish that can be served at room temperature, making it an excellent choice for buffets and potlucks. (Serves 6)

1 cup (240 mL) boiling water

$\frac{1}{2}$ cup (120 mL) sundried tomatoes (if packed in oil, rinse)

2 cloves garlic, peeled

1 Tbsp. (15 mL) herbes de Provence (mix of dried rosemary, thyme, savory, basil, and marjoram)

$\frac{1}{2}$ cup (120 mL) fresh parsley leaves

$\frac{1}{2}$ cup (120 mL) fresh basil leaves

$\frac{1}{3}$ cup (80 mL) olive oil

1 tsp. (5 mL) salt

1 cup (240 mL) water

1 cup (240 mL) couscous

3 cups (720 mL) roasted vegetables (see p. 58)

1 19 oz. (532 mL) can chickpeas, drained and rinsed

black olives for garnish (optional)

In a small bowl, pour boiling water onto the tomatoes and let them soak for 20 minutes. Drain, reserving the soaking water. Place the drained tomatoes in a food processor with the garlic, dry herbs, and $\frac{1}{2}$ cup (120 mL) of reserved soaking water. Process until quite smooth; then add the parsley, basil, olive oil, and salt. Process again and set this pesto aside. In a small saucepan, bring 1 cup (240 mL) water to a boil. Add the couscous. When the water returns to the boil, remove from heat, cover, and set aside for 5 minutes. Turn the couscous into a large bowl; fluff with a fork. Add the remaining soaking water and mix it in. Stir in half of the pesto. Add the vegetables, chickpeas, and remaining pesto and toss again. Adjust for salt. Serve at room temperature, garnished with olives if desired.

(Adapted from a recipe that appeared in Food and Drink, Autumn 1997.*)*

desserts

frosted chocolate cake

This cake packs a serious chocolate punch. Ideal for birthdays, or everyday chocoholics. (Makes two 8-in. [20 cm] layers)

3 cups (720 mL) all purpose flour
2 cups (475 mL) sugar
6 Tbsp. (90 mL) + 1 cup (240 mL) cocoa
2 tsp. (10 mL) baking soda
1 tsp. (5 mL) + ⅛ tsp. (.5 mL) salt
2 cups (475 mL) cold water
⅔ cup (160 mL) vegetable oil
2 Tbsp. (30 mL) white vinegar
2 tsp. (10 mL) + ½ tsp. (2.5 mL) vanilla
3 cups (720 mL) icing sugar
6 Tbsp. (90 mL) margarine
3 Tbsp. (45 mL) hot water (approx.)

Preheat the oven to 350°F (175°C). Sift and combine flour, sugar, 6 Tbsp. (90 mL) cocoa, baking soda, and 1 tsp. (5 mL) salt in a large bowl. In a separate bowl, combine the water, oil, vinegar, and 2 tsp. (10 mL) vanilla. Make a depression in the dry ingredients and mix in the wet ingredients. Beat until smooth. Grease two 8 in. (20 cm) round cake pans, and line bottoms with waxed paper. Pour the batter into the pans and bake for 30–40 minutes. Cool, then turn out the cakes, and slice each one into two layers.

Mix the icing sugar and remaining 1 cup (240 mL) cocoa together. Blend in margarine, $\frac{1}{2}$ tsp. (2.5 mL) vanilla and $\frac{1}{8}$ tsp. (.6 mL) salt. Add just enough hot water to give icing a spreadable consistency (not too much!). This makes enough frosting to cover the cake and three inside layers.

note:

If you want to vary the flavor for the internal layers, spread them with a thin layer of jam instead of chocolate frosting. Or add some instant coffee (dissolved in the hot water) to some or all of the frosting to make mocha-flavored frosting.

triceratopped spice cake

One cake—three different toppings. Your friends will marvel at the sudden explosion of your repertoire. (Makes one 8 in. [20 cm] square cake)

1 ½ cups (360 mL) all purpose flour
1 cup (240 mL) sugar
1 tsp. (5 mL) baking soda
1 tsp. (5 mL) cinnamon
½ tsp. (2.5 mL) allspice
½ tsp. (2.5 mL) salt
½ cup (120 mL) cold water
½ cup (120 mL) applesauce
⅓ cup (80 mL) vegetable oil
1 Tbsp. (15 mL) white vinegar
5 Tbsp. (75 mL) brown sugar
3 Tbsp. (45 mL) margarine
1 Tbsp. (15 mL) soymilk
½ cup (120 mL) shredded unsweetened coconut

Preheat the oven to 350°F (175°C). Sift and combine the flour, sugar, baking soda, cinnamon, allspice, and salt. In a separate bowl combine the water, applesauce, oil, and vinegar. Make a depression in the dry ingredients and mix in the wet ingredients. Beat until smooth. Pour into an ungreased 8 in. (20 cm) square pan. Bake for 30—40 minutes, until lightly browned on top. Cool, then leave in the pan to be iced.

In a small saucepan, bring the brown sugar, margarine, and soymilk to a boil. Remove from heat. Fold in the shredded coconut. Pour over cake.

alternative topping:
Spread a thin layer of raspberry or apricot jam over the top of the cake.

alternative topping:
Before baking the cake, cover the top with an overlapping layer of thinly sliced apples, peaches, or pears.

carrot fruitcake

A scrumptious cake for morning or afternoon tea time. So healthy we needn't count it as dessert. (Makes 1 loaf)

1 cup (240 mL) carrots, grated
1 cup (240 mL) raisins or currants
³⁄₄ cup (180 mL) rice syrup
1 ½ cups (360 mL) water
2 Tbsp. (30 mL) vegetable oil
1 tsp. (5 mL) cinnamon
1 tsp. (5 mL) allspice
1 tsp. (5 mL) salt
½ tsp. (2.5 mL) nutmeg
¼ tsp. (1.2 mL) cloves
1 ½ cups (360 mL) flour (all purpose, whole wheat, or a combination)
½ cup (120 mL) wheat germ
½ cup (120 mL) chopped walnuts
1 tsp. (5 mL) baking soda

Preheat the oven to 325°F (165°C). Combine the carrots, raisins, syrup, water, oil, and spices in a medium saucepan. Bring to a boil, then lower to simmer for 10 minutes. Remove the mixture from heat and allow it to cool. Combine the flour, wheat germ, walnuts, and baking soda in a large bowl. Mix in the carrot mixture. Pour batter into a greased loaf pan. Bake for 45 minutes.

banana surprise tea cake

A mouth-watering concoction I consider to be the perfect accompaniment to a steaming mug of lapsang souchong tea. If you prefer a healthier version, substitute ¹/₂ cup (120 mL) currants and ¹/₂ cup (120 mL) chopped walnuts for the chocolate chips and coconut.
(Makes 1 loaf)

3 very ripe bananas
juice of 1 lemon
¹/₂ cup (120 mL) brown sugar
¹/₂ cup (120 mL) vegetable oil
1 ¹/₂ cups (360 mL) whole wheat flour
¹/₂ cup (120 mL) wheat germ
¹/₂ tsp. (2.5 mL) each salt, baking powder, and baking soda
¹/₂ cup (120 mL) semi-sweet chocolate chips
¹/₂ cup (120 mL) unsweetened shredded coconut

Preheat the oven to 375°F (190°C). In a small bowl, mash the bananas and mix with lemon juice until they are smooth. Mix the sugar and oil together in a separate small bowl; then add to the banana mixture, stirring well. In a large bowl, combine the flour, wheat germ, salt, baking powder, and baking soda. Stir in the banana mix, chocolate chips, and coconut. Turn the batter into a greased loaf pan and bake for 40—45 minutes.

pain d'épices

A slice of "spice bread," lightly toasted, is a lovely addition to Christmas brunch. I make a couple of batches of this recipe because the baby loaves make perfect gifts. Let the bread ripen at room temperature for three days to maximize the flavor. (Makes 5 baby loaves)

2 cups (475 mL) mixed nuts (slivered almonds, skinned hazelnuts, walnuts, pine nuts, pecans)

1 cup (240 mL) dried mixed fruit (apricots, figs, prunes, and dates), diced

$1/_4$ cup (60 mL) currants

$1/_4$ cup (60 mL) light raisins

zest of 1 lemon

zest of 1 orange

4 tsp. (20 mL) baking soda

2 tsp. (10 mL) pastis (anise-flavored liqueur)

$1/_4$ tsp. (1.2 mL) each cinnamon, nutmeg, and ground cloves

pinch of salt

$1^3/_4$ cups (420 mL) water

1 cup (240 mL) rice syrup

$3/_4$ cup (180 mL) sugar

2 Tbsp. (30 mL) dark rum

3 cups (720 mL) all purpose flour, sifted

Preheat the oven to 350°F (175°C). Grease five aluminum baby loaf pans ($5^3/_4$ x $3^1/_4$ x 2 in./15 x 8 x 5 cm). Dust them with flour and tap out the excess. Place the pans on a baking sheet. In a large bowl, combine the nuts, mixed fruit, currants, raisins, and zest. Mix well. Add the baking soda, pastis, and spices. Stir to mix. In a medium saucepan over medium heat, combine the water, rice syrup, sugar, and rum. Bring to a boil, then remove from heat. Pour over the fruit and nut mixture and stir gently. Let it sit for 5 minutes, stirring occasionally. Add the flour, stir well, and let it sit for 3 minutes.

Divide the batter equally among the pans. Cover the pans with an aluminum foil tent. Place the baking sheet in the oven and bake for 40—45 minutes, until a toothpick inserted in the middle comes out just slightly moist. Cool the breads on a rack. Remove them from pans and wrap them in plastic. Let them ripen for three days at room temperature. To serve, cut the bread into thin slices. (Toasted slices are delicious!)

(Adapted from a recipe by François Payard in The New York Times.)

fresh fruit with maple cream

This delectable creamy topping turns fruit into dessert. Also delicious on granola. (Serves 4)

   12 oz. (340 g) silken tofu (silken tofu is essential for this recipe)
   ⅓ cup (80 mL) maple syrup
   ½ tsp. (2.5 mL) vanilla
   zest from 1 lemon or lime
   3 cups (720 mL) fresh berries, sliced peaches, or sliced kiwis
      (or a combination)

Combine the tofu, maple syrup, and vanilla in a food processor until smooth. Add the grated zest and stir. Spoon over fruit.

apple-cranberry maple crisp

A cranberry-enhanced version of the old standard. This makes a fitting conclusion to a Thanksgiving feast. (Makes one 8 in. [20 cm] square pan)

7 large Macintosh apples, peeled and sliced
1 cup (240 mL) apple juice or cider
$\frac{1}{2}$ cup (120 mL) cranberries
1 tsp. (5 mL) cinnamon
pinch of salt
1$\frac{1}{2}$ cups (360 mL) rolled oats
$\frac{1}{2}$ cup (120 mL) all purpose flour
$\frac{1}{2}$ cup (120 mL) chopped walnuts
$\frac{1}{4}$ cup (60 mL) vegetable oil
3 Tbsp. (45 mL) maple syrup

Preheat the oven to 350°F (175°C). Combine the apples, apple juice/cider, cranberries, cinnamon, and salt in an ungreased 8 in. (20 cm) square pan. To prepare the topping, combine the oats, flour, nuts, oil, and maple syrup in a bowl. Press the topping over the fruit mixture. Bake for 40 minutes. Let cool for 10 minutes before serving.

(Adapted from a recipe by Janet Campbell that appeared in the Merrickville Phoenix.)

peach and blueberry crisp

For summer nights when fruit alone won't suffice. Serve with a dollop of whipped topping. (Makes one 8 in. [20 cm] square pan)

8 large ripe peaches
1 cup (240 mL) fresh or frozen blueberries
$\frac{1}{2}$ cup (120 mL) + 1 Tbsp. (15 mL) brown sugar, packed
$\frac{3}{4}$ cup (180 mL) + 1 Tbsp. (15 mL) all purpose flour
$\frac{3}{4}$ cup (180 mL) quick-cooking oats
dash of salt
$\frac{1}{2}$ cup (120 mL) margarine

Preheat the oven to 350°F (175°C). Peel and slice the peaches. (If you can't peel them easily, scald them in a pot of boiling water for about 15 seconds. Then peel.) Combine the peaches and blueberries in an 8 in. (20 cm) square baking pan (ungreased). Add 1 Tbsp. (15 mL) brown sugar and 1 Tbsp. (15 mL) flour to the fruit and stir to combine. In a small bowl, mix all remaining ingredients except the margarine. Cut in the margarine with two knives, or work with fingers to make a crumbly mixture. Press the topping over the fruit. Bake for 35 minutes. Cool slightly.

banana-poppyseed muffins

This muffin recipe can be endlessly varied by adding different kinds of nuts, fruits, and/or berries. One of my favorite variations is to add the rind from an orange to the dry ingredients, and substitute juice from the orange for an equal amount of soymilk. (Makes 12 small muffins)

1 cup (240 mL) all purpose flour
1 cup (240 mL) whole wheat flour
2 Tbsp. (30 mL) sugar
$2\frac{1}{2}$ tsp. (12.5 mL) baking powder
1 tsp. (5 mL) egg replacer
$\frac{1}{2}$ tsp. (2.5 mL) salt
3 large ripe bananas, mashed
1 cup (240 mL) soymilk
$\frac{1}{2}$ cup (120 mL) fresh or frozen blueberries
$\frac{1}{4}$ cup (60 mL) vegetable oil
2 Tbsp. (30 mL) poppy seeds

Preheat the oven to 375°F (190°C). Sift the dry ingredients (except poppy seeds) into one bowl. Combine the bananas, soymilk, blueberries, and oil in a separate bowl. Make a well in the dry ingredients and add in the contents of the other bowl, mixing just enough to combine. Spray a muffin tin with vegetable oil spray. Spoon the mixture into the muffin tin, and sprinkle the tops of the muffins with poppy seeds. Bake for 15–20 minutes, or until a toothpick inserted in the center of one muffin comes out clean.

fried bananas with ginger and cloves

If you forgot dessert, don't panic. You can whip up fried bananas in about the time it takes to brew the coffee. This version is more spicy than sweet. (Serves 4)

3 Tbsp. (45 mL) brown sugar
3 Tbsp. (45 mL) apple juice
2 Tbsp. (30 mL) orange juice
2 tsp. (10 mL) fresh ginger, grated
1 tsp. (5 mL) orange or lemon zest
$\frac{1}{4}$ tsp.(1.2 mL) ground cloves
1 Tbsp. (15 mL) margarine or vegetable oil
4 firm bananas, peeled and sliced lengthwise in halves

Mix all ingredients except the margarine and bananas in a food processor until smooth. Heat the margarine over medium heat in a large frying pan. Place the bananas in the pan in a single layer. Cook for a few minutes, then turn them gently and brown them slightly on the opposite side. Pour the juice mixture overtop and cook until the bananas are heated through and the sauce is bubbly hot (about 5 minutes). Serve immediately, garnished with a bit of zest or a pinch of cinnamon (or nutmeg).

variation:

These bananas can be flambéed. Place the fried bananas on individual serving plates. Heat $\frac{1}{4}$ cup (60 mL) brandy in the frying pan. Light it. Pour over the bananas and serve immediately.

ice wine peaches

The best of the winter and summer harvests in a single dish. Delicious served with Almond Biscotti (see next page). (Serves 4)

4 peaches
2 tsp. (10 mL) sugar
½ cup (120 mL) ice wine

Place the peaches in a pot of boiling water for about 15 seconds, until you can remove the skins easily. Drain the peaches and remove the skin. Slice them into bite-sized pieces, arrange them in individual serving dishes, and sprinkle with ½ tsp. (2.5 mL) sugar per serving. Pour 2 Tbsp. (30 mL) wine over each serving and chill for at least ½ hour.

(Adapted from Rose Elliot's Vegan Feasts.)

almond biscotti

Biscotti ("twice baked") are easy and fun to make. The Italian way is to serve them with Vin Santo ("holy wine"), a sweet dessert wine, but I prefer to dip them in coffee or tea. (Makes approximately 20 biscotti)

2 cups (475 mL) all purpose flour
³⁄₄ cup (180 mL) sugar
³⁄₄ cup (180 mL) finely ground almonds
³⁄₄ cup (180 mL) whole unblanched almonds
¹⁄₂ tsp. (2.5 mL) baking soda
¹⁄₂ tsp. (2.5 mL) cinnamon
¹⁄₂ cup (120 mL) water
¹⁄₃ cup (80 mL) rice syrup

Preheat the oven to 350°F (175°C). Mix together the flour, sugar, almonds, baking soda, and cinnamon in a bowl. Stir in the water and syrup to make a very stiff dough. Divide the dough in half. Roll out each half into a 15 in. (38 cm) log shape. Place logs on a parchment-lined baking sheet, well spaced from one another. Bake for 30 minutes, until they are firm and golden. Remove the logs from the oven and cool them slightly. Then slice the logs on the diagonal, spacing cuts ¹⁄₂ in. (1.2 cm) apart. Return the biscuits to the oven and cook about 15 minutes longer, until they are dry and lightly colored.

 **variation:**
For almond-orange biscotti, add the zest and juice from 2 oranges to the batter. Omit the water.

(Adapted from a recipe developed by the Nick Malgieri Restaurant, Toronto.)

creamy chocolate-orange pudding

I make this pudding when kids (of any age) are coming for dinner. Escalate their enthusiasm to a fever pitch by decorating individual servings with a bit of whipped topping dusted with chocolate or coconut shavings, or jellybeans, or finely grated orange and lime rind with a pinch of nutmeg. (Serves 3—4)

12 oz. (340 g) silken tofu (silken tofu is essential for this recipe)
$\frac{1}{2}$ cup (120 mL) sugar
$\frac{1}{4}$ cup (60 mL) cocoa
2 Tbsp. (30 mL) orange juice
finely grated rind from 1 orange
1 Tbsp. (15 mL) oil
$\frac{1}{2}$ tsp. (2.5 mL) vanilla
$\frac{1}{8}$ tsp. (.5 mL) salt

Combine all ingredients in a blender or food processor until smooth and creamy. Chill and serve.

variation:

Omit the orange rind and juice to make plain chocolate pudding. Or dissolve $1\frac{1}{2}$ tsp. (7.5 mL) instant coffee in 1 Tbsp. (15 mL) hot water, and add to the basic chocolate pudding to make mocha pudding. Decorate with chocolate-covered espresso beans.

(Adapted from Louise Hagler's Tofu Cookery.*)*

green tea tofu ice cream

This tofu ice cream isn't as creamy as the commercially made varieties, but it has great color and a unique flavor. Can be served with additional kiwis for garnish. (Serves 4)

1 cup (240 mL) soymilk
4 green tea bags
12 oz. (340 g) silken tofu (silken tofu is essential for this recipe)
2 ripe kiwis, peeled and cut into chunks
1 cup (240 mL) rice syrup
1 Tbsp. (15 mL) vanilla
3—4 drops green food coloring
1 cup (240 mL) whipped topping

Place the soymilk and tea bags in a medium saucepan. Bring to a boil, then simmer for 5 minutes, stirring frequently. Remove from heat. Refrigerate for at least 20 minutes, but not more than an hour. Gently squeeze the absorbed milk out of tea bags and discard the bags. Put the tofu and kiwis in a food processor and process until smooth. Add the syrup, soymilk tea, vanilla, and food coloring. Process until thoroughly combined. Pour the mixture into a metal or plastic bowl. Gently fold the whipped topping into the mixture. Cover and freeze for 6—7 hours or until firm, giving the mixture a periodic stir to help it freeze more evenly.

(Adapted from a recipe by Ying Chang Compestine that appeared in Self, May 1998.)

a glossary of ingredients

asafoetida: A pungent, garlicky powder ground from the taproot of the giant fennel plant, used in Indian cooking. Available from Asian food stores.

barley: Comes in two types, pot barley and the more processed pearl barley. Pot barley takes longer to cook, but it has better texture, flavor, and nutrition.

bulgur: A quick-cooking cracked wheat that has been hulled and par-boiled.

cilantro/coriander: When a recipe calls for cilantro, use the fresh leaves of the coriander plant. When it calls for coriander, use the dry powder (made from the seeds of the plant).

couscous: A quick-cooking ground wheat (or semolina pasta) of North African origin.

egg replacer: A combination of starches and leavening agents that binds and leavens cooked and baked foods. Available from natural food stores. (Alternatively, you can replace an egg in baking with 1 Tbsp. [15 mL] ground flax seed.)

eggless mayonnaise: Made from tofu ("tofunaise") or other alternatives. Available from natural food stores and some grocery stores.

ginger: Many recipes in this book call for fresh ginger root. A tip for keeping ginger always on hand is to store it in the freezer. When you need some, just cut off a chunk or grate the required amount, and return the rest to the freezer.

margarine: See oils/margarine.

nutritional yeast: The best-quality nutritional yeast should be high in B vitamins (including B_{12}). Available from natural food stores. Can be stored in the freezer.

oils/margarine: My favorite all-purpose oil is olive oil. When using it in the early stages of a dish (e.g. for sautéeing) you don't need to use extra virgin. However, when it comes to dressing or finishing a dish, use a high-quality olive oil if you can. I also like to use flax seed oil because it's an excellent source of omega 3 fatty acids. It has to be stored in the fridge, and loses its nutritional value if cooked. I add a little bit to salad dressings or to finish cooked vegetables. Sesame oil comes in two types: light and dark. The recipes in this book call for the dark, or toasted, oil. Light varieties are used for sautéeing. Toasted sesame oil, which burns easily, is usually added after cooking as a flavor accent. In general I prefer to cook and bake with oils, saving margarine (non-hydrogenated) for spreading on bread or muffins. (Vegan margarine is available from health food stores.) For baking, I generally use cold-pressed canola oil (another good source of omega 3 fatty acids).

Patak's curry paste: Patak's wonderful selection of curry pastes and chutneys is widely available at supermarkets (usually the "international foods" section), as well as natural food stores, Asian food stores, etc. The curry pastes come in mild, medium, and hot varieties. They are an excellent base for any number of delicious vegetable curries. Simply sauté some onions, add a can of tomatoes, then add your favorite vegetables and 2–3 Tbsp. (30–45 mL) of curry paste. Cover and simmer until the vegetables are tender.

quinoa: A quick-cooking grain that looks like tapioca pearls when cooked. It was a staple food for the Incas, and is high in protein and calcium. Quinoa produces a natural coating called saponin to protect it from sun and pests. This protective layer is removed during processing, but you should give quinoa a good wash before using it to remove any residues. Available from natural food stores.

rice syrup: Less sweet than honey and other sweeteners, but an excellent alternative to them. Available from natural food stores.

Sambar powder: A South Indian "masala" (spice mixture) that includes black pepper, turmeric, coriander, fenugreek, and cumin. Available from Asian food stores.

soymilk: A beverage made from soy-beans. Available in whole and low-fat varieties, and several flavors (natural, vanilla, chocolate, straw-berry). Soymilk is an excellent source of protein and most varieties are fortified with vitamins D and B_{12}, as well as calcium. You can use soymilk as a substitute for cow's milk as a beverage, in tea and coffee, in "soy shakes," on cereal, in baking, and to make cream sauces.

tahini: A paste made from ground sesame seeds. This common ingredient in east Mediterranean foods is available from natural food stores and most grocery stores.

tamari: Concentrated soy sauce. Available in most grocery stores.

tempeh: A cultured food, high in protein, made from soybeans. It has a dense, chewy texture. Tempeh is sold frozen because it deteriorates quickly. It is available from natural food stores.

Thai green curry paste: A concentrated mixture of fresh green chilies and Thai spices. Available from Asian food stores and many regular grocery stores.

tofu: Or bean curd, is a cheese-like substance made from soymilk. It comes in two basic textures: silken or regular. Silken tofu is soft and creamy. It is commonly available fresh ("water-packed") or in vacuum-packed "aseptic" packages. I use silken tofu for puddings and dips, and sometimes for other recipes as well because the aseptic boxes are so easy to keep on hand. Silken tofu is sometimes called dessert tofu, and is also available ready-flavored and sweetened as a pudding-like dessert. Regular tofu is chewier, and ranges in density from soft to very firm. It is usually "calcium-set" (made with calcium), and therefore a good source of this nutrient (but check the ingredients label to be sure). Regular tofu is available in most grocery stores, usually "water-packed" in plastic tubs. The firmest varieties are best for recipes where you want the tofu to hold together (e.g. stir-fries). When using water-packed tofu, it should be pressed to remove excess water. Place it on a tea towel with a cutting board or other heavy object on top, and let it sit for about 15 minutes. Opened, unused tofu can be frozen, or kept in the fridge for a few days if it's covered regularly with fresh water. Tofu is quite high in fat (up to 40% of calories), so I sometimes use "lite" varieties, especially in desserts.

veggie bacon bits: Widely available in most grocery stores, usually in the herbs/spices/flavorings section.

menu planning

The recipes in this book are organized to facilitate menu planning. The dishes in the Main Dishes section are filling and provide the basis around which to build a meal. Think of them as the replacement for meat in a traditional menu. By adding bread and a green salad or a side vegetable or grain dish from the Side Dishes section, voilà, you have a well-rounded and satisfying meal.

Another good tip to keep in mind is to eat in season. Fresh berries are made for summer eating, whereas nothing is more pleasing on a cold January day than a spicy root vegetable soup. With imported foods available year-round in the supermarkets, we tend to forget the satisfaction that comes from eating cooler, lighter, fresher foods in summer and hotter and heavier foods (more fats and carbohydrates) in winter. The recipes in this book feature foods for all seasons.

Remember that color and texture are extremely important in our enjoyment of food. Provide as much variation as possible to create a pleasing palette. If you're serving a hot vegetable that's orange-colored, then a simple green salad on the side might be nice. But if you're serving a hot green vegetable, then a mixed salad with lots of color would make a better accompaniment. Different color groups of vegetables have different vitamins, so the more colorful your plate is, the more likely you're getting a beneficial range of nutrients.

It's also important to vary food textures and structure. A plate full of soft mushy foods (baked beans, mashed potatoes, steamed spinach) is less pleasing than one with more contrast (substitute a baked potato). Garnishes (fresh herbs, croutons, raw vegetables and fruits, toasted nuts and seeds) are a tried and true method for adding color or a bit of pleasing crunch. And finally, flavors also need to be varied, so if you're serving a main dish with orange flavor (such as Black Beans à l'Orange), then you should avoid an orange-flavored dessert. You get the idea.

On special occasions, my strategy is usually to add more dishes rather than just making more of a single main dish. For example, I might add one or two starters to the meal. Or I might make an extra main or side dish. I always choose several dishes that can be made ahead and reheated, or served at room temperature. The following menus are some of my favorites.

SUMMER LUNCH:

Chilled Cucumber Soup (prepare in advance), page 51

Tarragon Lentil-Nut Loaf (prepare in advance, serve at room temperature), page 88

Baked Red Peppers with Garlic and Capers, page 69

Green or Mixed Salad

Fresh Fruit with Maple Cream (prepare in advance, but don't mix fruit and cream together until ready to serve), page 132

SPECIAL OCCASION SUMMER DINNER:

Gazpacho (prepare in advance), page 50

Roasted Vegetable Couscous with Sundried Tomato Pesto (prepare in advance, serve at room temperature), page 121 or Pissaladière, page 116

Fresh Corn on the Cob

Green Salad

Green Tea Tofu Ice Cream, page 140, or Ice Wine Peaches (prepare in advance), page 137

WINTER LUNCH:

Hungarian Mushroom Soup, page 52, *or* Garlic Bread Soup (prepare
in advance, reheat), page 54

Red and White Onion Tart (prepare in advance, reheat), page 118

Quinoa Pilaff with Apricots and Currants, page 81

Green or Mixed Salad

Carrot Fruitcake, page 128, *or* Creamy Chocolate-Orange Pudding
(prepare in advance), page 139

SPECIAL OCCASION WINTER DINNER:

Pecan Mushroom Pâté served before dinner (prepare in advance),
page 44

Fennel and Apple Phyllo Triangles, page 46, *or* Artichokes with Herb
Vinaigrette, page 47

Black-Eyed Beans with Cumin, page 92, *or* Tangy Black Beans à
l'Orange (prepare in advance), page 93

Wild Rice Waldorf Salad (prepare in advance), page 67

Green Salad

Triceratopped Spice Cake, page 126, *or* Fried Bananas with Ginger and
Cloves, page 136 (cake can be prepared in advance, but not bananas)

EASIEST DINNER FOR A CROWD:

Kalamata Olive Tapenade, page 42, and/or White Bean and Herb
Spread, page 43 (prepare in advance)

Chili Sensation (prepare in advance), page 95

Mexican Corn Salad (prepare in advance), page 64

Fresh Bread and Green Salad

Frosted Chocolate Cake, page 124, *or* Apple-Cranberry Maple Crisp
(prepare in advance, reheat crisp), page 133

PICNIC SPECIAL

Tabouleh, page 66

Stuffed Grapevine Leaves, page 80

Grilled Tempeh, page 39, and/or Carrot-Tahini, page 39, sandwiches

Raw Vegetables/Pickles/Olives

Banana Surprise Tea Cake, page 129, *or* Carrot Fruitcake, page 128

vegan pets

I am sometimes reluctant to admit that my dog is vegan because I get some pretty hostile reactions. It's one thing to choose veganism for yourself, people say, but what right do you have to impose such an unnatural regime on a defenceless dog? It strikes them as the worst kind of fanaticism. How can such a practice be defended?

The first misconception to clear up is that, contrary to popular belief, dogs are not true carnivores. Like humans, they are adapted to eat plant and animal foods. Dogs require more protein than humans (approximately 15—25% of calories), and vegetarian dogs require a high calcium diet to balance the high phosphorous levels of a vegetable-based diet, but they can get these nutrients from either plant or animal sources. And like humans, they use carbohydrates as a primary source of energy.

Even when they're reassured that dogs can meet all of their nutritional requirements with a plant-based diet, some people worry that it's not "natural," and that dogs can't be satisfied with such a diet. It is a strange charge that a vegan diet is unnatural when you consider the canned food and kibble most people feed their pets. There is nothing natural about these products. Presumably, in a state of nature, dogs would be eating all of their food raw, not rendered, processed, and cooked. Furthermore, it seems unlikely that dogs would be dining often on domestic animals. In any case, the idea of a "natural" diet is a bit of a red herring. Dogs have been domesticated and bred by humans for centuries, eating what humans have chosen to feed them. It doesn't make sense to talk about "natural" dog food in this context.

It does, however, make sense to talk about meeting the nutritional requirements necessary for dogs to be happy and healthy (perfectly possible on a vegan diet). It also makes sense to talk about palatability—i.e. making food appealing to dogs so they enjoy their meals and maintain a healthy appetite. Just like humans, dogs are individual in their food likes and dislikes. Some dogs really love vegetables. They'll gobble up rice or raw carrots or broccoli with real gusto. Others will only eat foods with strong smells and flavors, but this needn't be meat or cheese. Dogs can't resist the slightly smoky flavor of imitation bacon bits and other vegetarian meat substitutes (veggie burgers and wieners, veggie pepperoni, etc.). They love tomato sauces, garlic, and go wild for the pungent cheesy smell/taste of nutritional yeast. (Cats really go for it too!) Once you've seen a dog's enthusiasm for these flavors, you won't worry that they are missing meat.

In addition to being nutritional and palatable, a vegan diet may be healthier for dogs (just as it is for humans) than many conventional diets. First of all, dogs on a vegan diet eat a portion of their food raw to ensure that they are getting sufficient enzymes, which are lost in the cooking process. These enzymes, important for healthy digestion, are lacking in conventional pet food. A second benefit is that vegan dog food is made from healthier ingredients than most conventional dog food. The rendered remains of domestic farm animals (typically diseased animals that fail the grade for human consumption) supply much of the protein and fat content of pet foods. As noted in the preface of this book, livestock are high on the food chain and thus concentrate significant amounts of pesticides and other chemicals in their bodies. Poisons are most concentrated in their organs (kidneys, liver, etc.), precisely those parts of the animal that often end up in pet food.

Our dog Codie (a lab-spaniel cross whom we adopted 11 years ago at age one) has been a vegan since we adopted him, and eats his vegan meals with enthusiasm. We have also noted that visiting meat-eating dogs are quite happy to eat Codie's food, especially the tomato and peanut butter-flavored dog treats. At age 12, our dog is a happy, healthy creature, with bright eyes, a vibrant coat, and oodles of energy. A further benefit of the diet is that one of its components, nutritional yeast, may provide some natural flea protection. Although we live in the country, and Codie has lots of exposure to other animals, we have never had a flea infestation and have never had to use flea collars, shampoos, or medications.

This is the good news. On the other hand, there is a time

commitment involved in feeding our dog a vegan diet. We make his food using a supplement called "Vegedog" developed by James and Barbra Peden. (For information about how to order the diet, please see the end of this section.) This means that once or twice a week we cook up a batch of rice, and mix it with soy protein, nutritional yeast, oil, veggie-dog supplement (mostly calcium and other minerals), and a bit of salt. At meal time we feed Codie this food, supplemented with some fresh vegetables. At first, making dog food seems like a pretty time-consuming task, but once you get yourself organized—buying suitable containers, buying ingredients in bulk, mixing the dry ingredients in large batches, cooking the rice when you're already in the kitchen doing something else—it's not a big deal. (We probably spend about 30 minutes a week making dog food and treats.) You also have to be more organized when you leave your dogs in someone else's care, whether you delegate the food making to them or make up extra food in advance.

Another option, of course, is to buy the commercially prepared vegetarian dog food now available from most pet food stores. My concern is that, as with all commercially prepared foods, it's hard to know about the quality of ingredients and the kinds of residues that might be present. By making homemade food we can ensure high-quality, fresh, whole, and, to some extent, raw foods. Over the years we have tried several vegetarian kibble foods, and have found that Codie likes them, but that he clearly prefers the homemade food. So we use some of both. The bulk of Codie's diet is homemade, but we also use some pre-fab kibble, especially when we're traveling, or otherwise unable to make his food.

I wouldn't expect you to make a radical change to your dog's diet on the basis of anecdotal evidence about our happy, healthy dog. But I do encourage you to do some reading and investigation of your own. *Vegetarian Cats and Dogs* by James Peden is an excellent introduction to this topic. I would also suggest finding a veterinarian who is supportive of vegetarian pet diets. A vet who advertises that he/she specializes in a holistic or homeopathic approach to pet care is probably a good place to start.

I have focused on vegan diets for dogs, because that is where I have first-hand experience. For all you cat lovers out there, you will be interested to know that many people have also maintained their cats on a vegetarian or vegan diet. Cats are true carnivores, and thus it is a far trickier proposition to meet their nutritional requirements (for protein and other nutrients) from a vegetable-based diet. For example, cats cannot make use of vegetable protein unless they have sufficient taurine in their diets. Most animals (including humans and dogs) produce this chemical in their bile, but cats do not. If they are not getting taurine through meat in their diet, they must take it as a supplement. Otherwise, a taurine deficiency will result in serious health problems. There are very few plant sources of taurine, but the "Vegecat" vegetarian cat supplement (see details at the end of this section) contains an adequate source. "Vegecat" also contains sources of vitamin A, niacin and arachidonic acid, all vital nutrients that cats cannot synthesize from plant sources the way dogs and humans can.

I can't overemphasize that if you decide to switch your dog or cat to a vegetarian diet, it's vital to use a veterinarian-approved diet. Concocting your own mix of soy, veggies, rice, etc. is bound to result in deficiencies. (For that matter, even if your pets are meat-eaters, you should follow an approved diet unless you are an expert in their nutritional needs.)

Our vegan dog is a constant source of joy and pride. He thrives on a vegan diet, and meanwhile we don't have to live with the strange contradiction of shunning meat ourselves while buying it to feed our dog. Our house is truly meat-free. Smelly, messy pet food tins—good riddance!

To order Vegedog or Vegecat supplements and recipes, contact:
Harbingers of a New Age
717 E. Missoula Ave.
Troy, MT 59935-9609
Phone: (406) 295-4944
Email: info@vegepet.com
Website: www.vegepet.com

resources for further reading

Adams, Carol J. and Josephine Donovan (Eds.) *Animals and Women: Feminist Theoretical Explorations*. Durham, NC: Duke UP.

Cavalieri, Paola. *The Animal Question: Why nonhuman animals deserve human rights*. Oxford and New York: Oxford UP, 2001.

Davis, Brenda, Victoria Harrison and Vesanto Melina. *Becoming Vegetarian: The complete guide to adopting a healthy vegetarian diet*. Toronto: Macmillan Canada, 1994.

Davis, Brenda and Vesanto Melina. *Becoming Vegan: The complete guide to adopting a healthy plant-based diet*. Summertown, TN: The Book Publishing Company, 2000.

Elliot, Rose. *The Vegetarian Mother and Baby Book*. New York: Pantheon, 1986.

Fox, Michael Allen. *Deep Vegetarianism*. Philadelphia: Temple University Press, 1999.

Lappé, Frances Moore. *Diet for a Small Planet*. New York: Ballantine Books, 1982.

Marcus, Erik. *Vegan: The New Ethics of Eating*. Ithaca: McBooks Press, 1998.

Masson, Jeffrey Moussaieff and Susan McCarthy. *When Elephants Weep: The Emotional Lives of Animals*. New York: Delacourt Press, 1995.

Peden, James A. *Vegetarian Cats and Dogs*. Harbingers of a New Age, 1995.

"Position of the American Dietetic Association: Vegetarian Diets," in *Journal of the ADA*. Vol. 97. No. 11 (November 1997), pp. 13—17.

Regan, Tom. *The Case for Animal Rights*. Berkeley: University of California Press. 1983.

Reinhardt, Mark Warren. *The Perfectly Contented Meat-Eater's Guide to Vegetarianism*. New York: Continuum, 1998.

Rifkin, Jeremy. *Beyond Beef: The Rise and Fall of the Cattle Culture*. New York: Dutton, 1992.

Robbins, John. *Diet for a New America: How Your Food Choices Affect Your Health, Happiness, and the Future of Life on Earth*. Walpole, NH: Stillpoint, 1987.

Singer, Peter. *Animal Liberation*. New York: Avon Books. 1975.

useful websites

NUTRITION
www.pcrm.org (Physicians Committee for Responsible Medicine)
www.strongbones.org (a PCRM site)
www.vegetariannutritiondpg.org (American Dietetic Association site)

ANIMAL RIGHTS
www.peta.org (People for the Ethical Treatment of Animals)
www.goveg.com (a PETA site)
www.animalconcerns.org
www.meat.org

TRAVEL

www.vegtravel.com

www.vegdining.com

www.ivu.org (International Vegetarian Union)

www.vegansociety.com (Vegan Society, UK)

ANIMAL INGREDIENTS

www.vrg.org/nutshell/faqingredients.htm

www.ivu.org/faq

VEGETARIAN PETS

www.vegepet.com

GENERAL

www.vegetariancentral.org

www.vegnews.com

www.vegetariantimes.com (*Vegetarian Times* magazine site)

www.veggielife.com (*Veggie Life* magazine site)

www.vrg.org (Vegetarian Resource Group)

www.vegsource.com/recipe

www.veg.on.ca (Toronto Vegetarian Association Site)

index